"I have personally known Rus[...] tual ministry focus has always bee[...] [...] love God, to live as a faithful follower of Jesus Christ under the influence of the indwelling Holy Spirit, and to understand what the Bible states regarding stewardship, debt, and all financial matters.

"Debt creates bondage, and that bondage comes in many forms and degrees. Just ask the people who have experienced divorce, broken relationships, and failed businesses. Today, experiencing the crushing pressure and life-changing impact of debt is starting much earlier in age—during college!

"Russ clearly spells out ways to avoid or reduce college debt. This is a must-read for every parent with children headed to college, every high school student considering college, and even students already in college. It is never too late to learn and apply God's biblical principles, apply wise applications, and experience the freedom of being debt-free."

David Bragonier, Barnabas Financial Ministry

"Most books on funding your education are about obtaining student loans or how to pay them off. Russ' insightful book is far better— how to get an education without debt! I highly recommend it!"

Chuck Bentley, CEO, Crown Financial Ministries
Author, Money Problems, Marriage Solutions

"Students often fail to comprehend the implications of insurmountable debt and the consequences of defaulting on their loans. Dr. Stevens offers practical and biblically sound advice on how to approach the subject of borrowing to attend college. He has developed tools and resources that provide step by step guidance on how to analyze spending and practice wise stewardship. Those who implement his strategy of becoming debt-free and exercise self-discipline in managing their finances will be thanking him for many years."

Dr. John Derry, President Emeritus of Hope International Univ.,
VP for Academic Affairs of Dallas Christian College

"Dr. Russell Stevens offers a timely and powerful book amid millions of people drowning in financial debt. Financial literacy has many biblical concepts and spiritual principles. Too many people of faith neglect their monetary responsibilities and walk blindly into financial debt. *Say No! to College Debt* highlights informative ways to obtain an educational degree without venturing into financial disasters. This book should be used by high school counseling offices, college counseling offices, students pursuing a college education, and families navigating the college financial matrix."
Dr. Ken J. Walden, President-Dean,
Gammon Theological Seminary

"Here's practical, street-level advice."
Marvin Olasky, Editor in chief, WORLD

"Russ Stevens has been a voice of encouragement and light to students who are struggling with making good financial decisions. Russ has a heart for helping young adults make good choices that lead to a great, purpose-filled life. This book is helpful in that it moves easily between broad themes and very practical advice and skills to help folks manage both their thinking and their day in and day out financial choices and responsibilities. This book would be a great gift for your kids and grandkids—anyone who needs honest, no nonsense suggestions on how to take care of the resources they possess."
Paul H. Alexander, Ph.D., President, Hope International Univ.

"College decisions continue to grow more difficult as prices have soared, and significant debt has become the norm. Russ Stevens has put together a concise, useful guide for sorting through the inevitable college-related questions. Readers will find helpful advice on everything from deciding whether going to college is the right choice to choosing the best school, and from paying for college *without* debt to getting *out* of debt if loans are unavoidable. If you're considering college for yourself or your children, this book will be a helpful resource."
Mark Biller, Executive Editor, Sound Mind Investing

Say No to College Debt

Discover How to Graduate Free of Loans
and Eliminate the Debt You Have Accumulated

Russell Stevens, CMA, MBA, Ph.D.

DEAR SOMER,   8/20
    I DOUBT YOU ARE HEADED
BACK TO COLLEGE. BUT I THOUGHT
YOU'D ENJOY THIS ANYWAY.
        LOVE
        [signature]

RIVER BIRCH PRESS

Daphne, Alabama

Note on Resource Availability

You'll find references to tools and resources scattered throughout the text and appendices. These will help you in your journey to becoming debt free. Many of these references are in too-small-to-use versions. Larger and computer-compatible versions of referenced forms and tools are available at www.SayNoToCollegeDebt.com. Along with the forms, you'll find links to videos that will help you understand how to use some of the tools.

Www.SayNoToCollegeDebt.com offers an additional set of videos on financial principles that teach us how God would have us live our financial lives. I also have a blog, which includes updates that will add value to the principles discussed in this book. The blog will allow us to explore more in-depth college-funding topics and will add new content as the college-funding scene changes. And as we all know, the only thing that won't change in life is the fact that there will be change.

ISBN 978-1-951561-34-5 (Print)
ISBN 978-1-951561-35-2 (Ebook)
For Worldwide Distribution
Printed in the U.S.A.

River Birch Press
P.O. Box 868
Daphne, AL 36526

To my wife, Kathy.
Without her support and patience,
I could never have gotten where I am
or done what has been done.
She has been more than a blessing
to me for over 38 years.

Contents

Acknowledgments

John Donne said, "No man is an island." This is especially true for authors. Sure, we spend a lot of solo time in front of a computer doing research and writing. But there are those upon whom we depend to help us finish the process. Besides Kathy, my patient and supporting wife, I'd like to thank a number of friends who agreed to read through the manuscript to give me suggestions. They included Dave and Debbie Bragonier, Doug and Robin Michaels, Chad and Stephanie Cunningham, Chuck Bentley, Kirk Blankenship, Ken Walden, Alan Rabe, and Steve Gardner. I also received some very effective advice in connecting with an agent and publisher from Kristy Woodson Harvey, Joel Belz, Marvin Olasky, Nat Belz, Steve McKinzie, Joseph Slife, and Jim Hart. Thanks to all of you for believing in me and sharing your time and expertise.

Many thanks to Keith Carroll for agreeing to represent me and finding a publisher. Your patience in dealing with a neophyte in book publishing has been a godsend.

I would be remiss to not acknowledge our sovereign God's guidance and support in bringing me to the point where this project was not only possible but has come to fruition. All praise and glory to Jesus Christ, my Lord.

Preface

This book offers hope to those who feel they live in a hopeless plight. Current news regularly reports the difficulties of taking on too much debt to get through college. You won't see hope in the newspapers or in the rhetoric of the politicians who try to use the crisis for political gain. But there is hope, as well as answers and solutions, if you know where to find them. You can complete college without going into the bondage of student loans. By applying some basic money principles, you can get out of your post-graduation debt quagmire. Please read on to see how to get a college education without debt and how to deal with any debt you may already have.

Debt is not inevitable. There are good, legitimate ways to get through college without borrowing money. If you're already in debt, you can pay it down now, whether or not you completed your degree.

This book is designed to help future students, current students, graduates, those who didn't graduate—and the parents and grandparents—to get out of the bondage that comes from borrowing large sums of money to pay for post-secondary schooling.

I challenge you to graduate from college debt free. I lived this challenge myself and had zero college debt when I graduated with each of my college degrees. The more I read and teach the principles from the Bible, which are contained in this book, the more I'm convinced that God's best for His people is to live debt free. I urge you to take up the challenge and start living without the bondage of college debt.

Introduction

In 2017, about 70 percent of the three million graduating high school seniors went straight to college.[i] Whether or not to go to college is up to the individual, but as an academic, I think a college education is a good thing.

When I was in high school, a diploma was the minimum qualification for a decent job. In today's technological world, most companies now require a bachelor's degree for entry-level jobs. And if applicants want a position in the upper levels of many of today's corporations, they need a master's degree or a doctorate.

The value of a good education includes more than just a job. George Washington Carver said, "Education is the key to unlock the golden door of freedom."[ii] While many think that applies only to oppressed minorities, it's true for everyone. If nothing else, a student will learn the discipline required to complete his or her schooling successfully. Discipline is a valuable tool in life.

For many students and future students, foregoing college isn't an option. Both the students and their families expect them to go. However, the cost is prohibitive for most people. If your family is wealthy, paying for college is not an issue. If your family is very poor, you can look into need-based scholarships and grants, which are available in abundance. The how-to-pay-for-college problem exists for the rest of the population—those who fall between the two extremes.

Many parents don't make enough money to pay tuition and fees, but they earn too much for their student to qualify for need-based scholarships and grants. The question then becomes, "Do I go to college?" If the answer is yes, the next question is, "How do I pay for it?" On the surface, that is what this book is about.

Many other forms of education are available for those who choose not to attend college or university. This book will touch on vocational and trade schools that enable students to learn a skill or enter a profession. These schools are a great way to learn the specific skills needed in many vocations. Jobs that require a college education are not the only way to be productive and earn a living.

For example, I thank God for the excellent mechanics who keep our car running. They may have learned on the job or at a technical school. Their work is not only meaningful but honorable. The same is true for the skilled men and women who fix things on our house, keep the power on, keep water flowing, and provide other services vital to our community. Skilled work is a viable and lucrative option for many high school graduates.

Career decisions interest God very much. He cares about our decisions and wants the best for us. And He is in charge of everything. We'll expand this concept in chapters one and eight. Keep God's plan for your life in mind as you read on.

ONE

Foundational Concepts

Much of the content we'll discuss is based on God's principles as presented in the Bible. That doesn't mean the principles won't work for someone who is not a believer or someone who is only considering believing in Christ. These are eternal principles found not only in the Bible, but also in some of the world's other great faith and wisdom literature.

God is in charge of everything. He cares about our decisions. These ideas lead directly to the concept of biblical stewardship.

Biblical stewardship goes one step beyond God merely being in charge of everything. It points to the logical conclusion that God owns everything. Chapter eight will contain more details on this. However, it's important to understand that grasping the concept of God owning everything is revolutionary. With God as the owner, all we do is manage what belongs to Him. This includes our talents, our natural giftedness, our past, our future, and even the decisions we make as we move through life.

Understanding biblical stewardship gives us great relief. It means the Lord cares about what I do as well as caring for me. Instead of fretting about the big decisions, my job is to determine what God wants for me. I also know He forgives and will make things right when I mess up. The Bible says, "And we know that in all things God works for the good of those who love him, who have been called according to his purpose" (Romans 8:28). He works for our good.

I have a wonderful relationship with God, and He wants to have a wonderful relationship with you too. God has given me strength to get through many dark days and joy in the good times. Because of my relationship with God, I get to spend eternity with Him, and I also have Him as my guide and support for my daily journey. God wants everyone "to come to a knowledge of the truth" (1 Timothy 2:4). You can also have this journey and receive His guidance, support, and joy. You will see much more on this topic in chapter nine's section on prayer.

TWO

Before You Sign Up for College

Should You Go to College?

First, ask yourself whether you need or desire to go to college to fulfill your calling in life. Not all vocations require college, but many do. For example, "lighting designers, sound engineers, and plumbers can jump right into an apprenticeship."[1]

Some children think they'll succeed in sports and won't need an education. The statistics show otherwise. Of the gifted athletes coming out of high school, some will get scholarships and play in a college setting. Of those successful in college, the NCAA estimates a very small percentage will make it into the professional ranks. The highest percentage (9.5 percent) of college athletes moving to the major leagues is in baseball.[2] The lowest (from the same study) is in basketball at 0.9 percent. Overall, only 30 out of 100,000 (0.03 percent) of high school basketball players make it to the pros.[3]

Even professional athletes don't spend their entire lives in sports. In football, the average tenure in the major leagues is 3.3 years.[4] Injuries take out many athletes early in their careers. People who make their living doing physical work, including athletics, age faster. Many don't last long in the athletic ranks for many reasons.

Some people think they'll be the next Bill Gates or Steve Wozniak. But we can count the number of uber-successful entrepreneurs on not-too-many fingers. Getting into that group is rare. And don't forget, even Bill Gates, Steve Wozniak, and other successful entrepreneurs had significant college time before leaving school to start their companies.

That's not to say there aren't jobs available for someone who wants to work hard and doesn't mind getting dirty. If those are your goals, then college is probably not for you. But if you want to get paid for what you know rather than what you do, you will probably need a good college education.

With those thoughts in mind, the decision to go to college or not is personal. It involves much thought, consideration, and prayer. Of the three, prayer is the most important. Proverbs 3:5–6 gives a good guide, "Trust God from the bottom of your heart; don't try to figure out everything on your own. Listen for God's voice in everything you do, everywhere you go; he's the one who will keep you on track" (MSG).[5] I will discuss prayer more extensively in chapter nine.

It's also a great idea to seek counsel; in fact, it's God's idea. I've listed scriptures about seeking counsel in the Scripture Appendix. Include your parents, grandparents, school counselors, pastors, and other wise people in the decision on whether to attend college. Remember, you're seeking counsel, but you don't have to follow all of it. But if you don't seek counsel, you'll miss out on a lot of valuable input. The missed input could make a huge difference in your future.

Pastor, professor, and theologian Richard Foster spoke of "meetings of clearness" in his book *The Freedom of Simplicity.*[6] A meeting of clearness involves bringing together people you respect. You then share your potential decision to gain "clearness" on the issue by seeking the mind of Christ. Prayerful input from people who have your best interest in mind is powerful. The decision may not pop up right away, but "without counsel plans fail, but with many advisers they succeed" (Proverbs 15:22, ESV).

There's no question these are tough decisions. But national research shows the unemployment rate for college-educated twenty-two- to twenty-seven-year-olds is just 4 percent, while the rate for the same age range without a college degree is 8.5 percent.[7] A number of years of college can make a big difference in getting and keeping a job. There is certainly no guarantee. But luck has often been defined as being in the right place at the right time with the right resume. College is certainly a positive portion of a good resume.

A number of years of college can make a big difference in your income. CNN Money reported college graduates will earn 67 percent more than those without degrees.[8] The article also said the average college graduate will earn enough by age thirty-four to make up for the time taken out of the workforce to go to school plus the cost of earning the degree. They'll make up for income lost during college years by the age of thirty-four. Beyond that, they will earn more than they would have without the degree.

According to the Department of Education, "over the course of a lifetime, the average worker with a bachelor's degree will earn approximately $1 million more than a worker without a postsecondary education. By 2020, an estimated two-thirds of job openings will require postsecondary education or training."[9] These are overall statistics. But they show the value of a college degree or advanced technical training.

It might be worth the time to do a cost-benefit analysis, comparing the costs of four or six years of college to the extra amount you would have earned if you'd worked instead of going to college. The process is basic, and the appendix has instructions on how to do a cost-benefit analysis. The directions include an example that analyzes a student who is good with numbers and thinking about an accounting degree.

If you need someone to help you with this, seek assistance from a local CPA, certified financial analyst, or the like. They would probably do this for a minimal fee.

Before leaving this topic, another quote from *Freedom of Simplicity* is in order. Many colleges and schools promote their graduates as highly successful and earning big money. Richard Foster addressed that motivation:

> Do we see a college education, for example, as a ticket to privilege or as a training for service to the needy? What do we teach our teenagers in this matter? Do we urge them to enter college because it will better equip them to serve? Or do we try to bribe them with promises of future status and salary increases? No wonder they graduate more deeply concerned about their standard of living than about suffering humanity.[10]

Analyze your motivation for going to college and plan accordingly. Is the goal to make a lot of money and then live in luxury for the rest of your life, or are you truly concerned for the less fortunate around you? There is much need in this world, and God might have chosen you to help meet some of that need. In chapter nine, you'll see how generosity is a no-lose situation.

Choosing What to Study

You should decide what to study before choosing and committing to a college or technical school. You'll decide what to study after you choose your major. Switching majors is expensive. I want to keep your college expenses down, so I want to help you avoid changing majors. Entrepreneur and best-selling author Ryan Holiday said college is "a very expensive place to find yourself."[11]

Regrettably, high school typically doesn't prepare graduates to know what they want to do in life. There are exceptions, but high school is designed to provide a broad spectrum of education rather than to help determine a career choice. One person said, "High school is there to prepare students for the adult world, to become good citizens, to learn a variety of subjects and to learn critical thinking."[12] Those are all important parts of determining a future career. But they won't help you choose and prepare for that career.

If you are ready to go to college but don't know what you want to do with your life, you can find tools to help you decide. Most of them require payment, but they are worth the initial expense because they save money on tuition and books you might have used pursuing directions that don't fit your calling and giftings.

These tools are personality testing and vocational testing. They determine how you react to things, what you like to do, and what you're good at. Most of them consist of questions about your preferences and can include dozens to hundreds of questions. Some even consist of multi-day assessments. You may think the more questions you answer, the more accurate the results, but that's not always the case. The longer tests are usually more expensive, but multiple questions are not a guarantee of a more accurate result. Like most purchases (and this is an important one), you need to research the product before buying and use the one with which you are the most comfortable.

There is also a difference between personality testing and vocational testing. Personality testing measures your personality profile. Vocational testing measures vocational aptitudes. A personality test might help to determine if you would be a good accountant. Typically, accountants are detail oriented and can work on a problem until it is done. Personality testing could help you determine if that would be a good choice for you or if it would be a disaster.

An example of vocational testing might be to determine how

good your spatial recognition is. If you were thinking of becoming a mechanical engineer, you would need to be able to look at a part or a drawing of a part and rotate it in your mind to see where it might fit with another part. This example would be something of a 3D jigsaw puzzle. Mechanical engineering might not be easy for you if you didn't have that ability.

Personality tests can help point you in appropriate directions. After that, vocational testing can help eliminate some of the directions that might not work for you. You'll find a discussion of personality and vocational testing resources in the appendix.

The Money Management for College Students workbook lists some reasons to choose a college major.[13] Some are poor and some wise. The poor reasons included:
1. Because the resulting job will make a lot of money.
2. Because the major will lead to a "hot job."
3. Because your parent specialized in this career field.
4. Because that's what your friends are pursuing.

The wise reasons consisted of:
1. To wrestle with your purpose in life. Rarely do those coming out of high school understand their purpose.
2. To clarify your purpose and take inventory of your God-given talents. These fit right into the personality and career testing already discussed above.
   a. Your personality will determine what you might be good at and what will bring a sense of fulfillment in the future.
   b. Your skills will determine a starting place. Remember, skills can be learned and can be added. Just because you can't fly a plane in high school, this doesn't rule out the possibility of a job as an airline pilot.
   c. Vocational interests may change throughout your career, but you need to start somewhere. If you're good with

      people, a social services career might be a good target.

  d. Work priorities and values are probably more important than the above items. While a good work ethic and Bible-based values probably won't get you your first job, they should ensure that you keep it and will pave the way for future jobs and promotions. Employers look for people they can trust. Trustworthy employees usually move up the ladder into more responsible positions or to good positions at other companies.

3. What subjects did you like in school? You'll probably be good in these areas in the long run. If you were good at English, you might consider a career in teaching, journalism, editing, or secretarial work.

With these suggestions in mind, move on to choosing a college that will help you accomplish what you consider your God-given direction, based upon the aptitudes, attitudes, and giftings God has given you.

THREE

Choosing a College or University

Before getting into the specifics of the college choices in front of you, the *Money Management for College Students workbook*[14] includes a list of considerations when choosing a college. I'll address some of them in later chapters. The list includes:

- Academic competitiveness of the school
- Strength of the school in your chosen academic major
- Urban versus rural setting
- Proximity to home
- Class size
- Cost
- Christian versus secular
- Safety
- Residence
- Graduate placement
- Specialty programs
- Tradition and family ties

While the academic competitiveness and strength of the school may seem minor, some professions will almost require making the right choice on those characteristics. While this is a rather elite example, the US Supreme Court limits your choice of law schools, should you want to become a Supreme Court judge. It's not a rule, but all Supreme Court justices have graduated from one of a small number of law schools.

Choosing a school close to home can save a lot of money in many ways. If your school is close enough, you can live at home and commute. And the school environment (urban versus rural) could influence your concentration on your classwork. Urban settings can be invigorating, but they can also pose significant distractions. Try to avoid getting into something that will keep you from your classwork. Academic success is the key. Good restaurants and theaters are not.

Christian versus secular is a big issue. Many students who were raised in the church go to a secular school, where their faith is not only ignored but may often be ridiculed. Even at a Christian school, your faith will be challenged. So make the right choice and be ready.

Safety is also a big concern. Few schools have walls around them, and people coming on campus can be threatening. Check with your admissions advisor to determine how the school will keep you physically safe on campus. If you want to be emotionally safe and not challenged in your beliefs, you may want to rethink going to college. Traditional teaching at college is more than just academics. It also helps a student learn how to think. If your beliefs are not challenged at college, you'll miss experiences that will support you in the real world beyond college.

Be sure to check out the dorms before you choose your school. Money is tight for many traditional campus-oriented schools. If the school of your choice keeps costs down by neglecting dorm repairs, rethink living in the dorms. Deferred maintenance in a dorm or classroom could result in illness, injury, or worse.

Graduate placement is the school helping you to find work. It's nice to have a degree. But if you can't find a job, the degree is not worth a lot. Does the school have a career-placement office to assist you to find a job? Does the placement office have a good record of finding good, appropriate jobs for their graduates?

Do you need a specialty program? I have a friend who does speech therapy for elementary-age students. That program isn't offered at every college. Be sure to look at specialty programs if you need them.

The last item on the list is tradition and family ties. Did your mom, dad, or grandparents go to a specific school and expect you to go there? Having a relative who has graduated from the school could be important for you and could cut the cost of your education. It's not uncommon for children and grandchildren of graduates to get a discount. Take the time to find out where your family went to school.

With an idea of what might be good for you and your future vocation, you now need to choose a college or a vocational/technical school. Author, editor-in-chief of *World Magazine*, and distinguished professor Marvin Olasky said, "The right college for a Christian is not one that will merely strengthen his resume. It is one that will go the furthest in strengthening heart, soul, and mind."[15] For many, this will not make any sense, but for those who try to implement the principles of biblical stewardship, Dr. Olasky hit the nail right on the head. Most colleges and universities teach skills and help students to mature. But learning how to think and cultivate wisdom and virtue are more expansive goals. Learning wisdom, virtue, and how to think will help a Christian student to develop a basis for life. Skills have less value when they are not based on good character. Keep this in mind as you choose, and you will learn to follow the direction God has for you, not the world's idea of how you should live.

Vocational/Technical School

At a vocational/technical school, you can get your needed skills by taking vocation-specific classes and skipping the cost of general-education classes. But then you'll miss out on significant learning about the world and the culture, which could have enhanced the rest of your life.

One definition of a vocational school is "any educational institution that is specifically geared toward helping students get employment-ready skills and knowledge for particular occupations."[16] An internet search on vocational schools at the time of this writing resulted in a list of over two hundred programs at schools all over the US and Canada.

Most vocational schools are private schools, so graduation requirements vary. However, some vocational schools tie into state college systems. The private schools are typically for-profit and require careful vetting before a student commits and sends money. Over the past decade, many big-name vocational schools have closed and left students with loans they still need to pay, even though they couldn't complete their degrees or certificate programs. See the section in chapter eight on paying off your debt if your college closed while you were enrolled.

If your chosen calling or vocation requires skills, but not necessarily a college degree, a vocational school may be a perfect fit. However, you still have to pay for the schooling. I'll address this in an upcoming chapter.

Four-year College or University

The majority of high school graduates who go to college will go straight to a four-year college or university. However, community colleges can save you a lot of money and can give you an idea of what you might be happy doing the rest of your life.

There are some distinct advantages to going straight to a four-year school. One big reason for choosing a four-year school is the fact that few, if any, community colleges teach their courses from a religious perspective. If your desire is to go to a school where classes are mostly taught from a religious worldview, you will probably need to go to a four-year school directly out of high school (or after a working gap year—see the discussion on gap years in chapter four under Personal Savings). Regrettably, going to a Christian school does not guarantee a Christian education. Some church-related schools operate with pretty much the same worldview as secular ones do. Investigate to be sure your choice of schools offers what you're seeking relating to worldview.

Professor Neil Kokemuller covered some more everyday benefits of going straight to a four-year school.[17] He started by highlighting the breadth of education available at a four-year school. Considering the size of some of the state-supported community colleges, this may not always be true. But it's a point worth investigating if you have a specific goal in mind.

He also highlighted the idea of getting a broader college experience outside the classroom. It's almost comical that he used movies and TV shows as examples of what happens on the campus of a four-year school and states that a student might want to be part of that. The entertainment industry rarely creates true documentaries of life on college campuses. It creates fiction to entertain. We shouldn't use the entertainment media as a measurement of how things will be at school.

Granted, every four-year residential school has on-campus activities, clubs, sports, and other extracurricular opportunities. But those activities also exist on community college campuses. Those activities help you to grow socially, culturally, and intellectually on whatever campus you attend class. The exception would be online schooling. But even online schools have social, cultural, and intellectual opportunities.

Professor Kokemuller discussed a smoother transition from your lower-division (freshman and sophomore years) to your upper-division (junior and senior years) work. This transition can be stressful but doesn't need to be. Changing campuses in the middle of your college career can be stressful, and he argued that starting on the four-year campus would eliminate that stress. That could be true. But isn't part of the purpose of college to prepare you for real life, in which job changes or transfers could involve a lot more than packing up an apartment or a dorm room and moving into another? Keep in mind that you could make payments for a long time to earn the luxury of not moving between your sophomore and junior years. How long you will pay will depend on the difference between the costs of the schools and the financing you have. The costs of all those extra expenses are explained in more detail in the following chapters.

Overall, there are good reasons to go to a community college before going on to finish at a four-year school. However, there may be great reasons to go straight to a four-year school. I want to help you hold down your costs and avoid overloading in debt. The decision is up to the student and his or her parents.

Community College

Most states in the US have excellent community college systems. There students can complete many required general education courses at a much cheaper rate than they would pay at a four-year college, public or private. Community colleges are also not as rigorous in their selections of students. If you had issues in high school and didn't graduate with a sufficient GPA for acceptance into a four-year college, a community college can give you a fresh start toward transferring to a selective four-year college. Spend your first two years at your community college and do your best work there. Transferring to a four-year college will be much easier with a great transcript from the community college. Your high school grades will fade into the past if you have recent grades showing significant improvement.

Most community colleges also offer some of the vocational programs addressed in chapter three. Besides, going to a community college could also allow you to live at home, thereby saving money on housing and food. While staying at home as you start college may seem oppressive, starting life with no debt is a goal worth sacrificing for.

Community colleges also give the opportunity to study alongside students of your own age and older students, who have gained significant life experience and are coming back for more education. Many will share their experiences with you so you can learn what a particular vocation might entail. Community colleges also employ instructors who have experience in the work world relating to the classes they teach. Instructors with real work experience can add to the education's value. With the pressure on four-year colleges to employ instructors with doctoral degrees, instructors with work experience in their field can be less available to the students at four-year colleges.

One interesting advantage of the community college is that most employers don't care where you earned your degrees. For those who do care, the place where you finished your bachelor's degree is the most important. For most employers, any good college is fine for your bachelor's degree. You might get some raised eyebrows if your degree is from a foreign school. But unless you have a very technical degree, like an MD, most employers probably will not care if your degree is from a foreign school.

The community college is also a great place to go if you don't yet know what you want to do for the rest of your life. It's not uncommon to meet a first-year student or a sophomore in college who doesn't yet know their life's direction. Taking your general education classes at a less-expensive school will allow you time to get a better idea of your future calling. Local community colleges typically offer personality and vocational testing to help you determine where your interests and skills would lead. You will want to avail yourself of this service during your first year at the community college.

Before you start your second year, you should apply at colleges where you hope to transfer. In some states, finishing an AA degree at a community college guarantees your acceptance into one of the state's four-year colleges or universities. You may not get admitted to the campus of your choice, but you will get into a state four-year college or university.

If you have direction for your future before starting college, decide what classes you want to take in your junior and senior year. This will help you choose your classes at the community college for your freshman and sophomore years. Knowing where you're heading also helps you to decide what college you want to attend at the end of your community college career. The advantage is that advisors at your target college will let you know what they will require for transfer. Sometimes a college will take all your credits from the community college and apply them toward your four-year degree. Sometimes, it's better to complete an AA degree at the community college and take that into the four-year college. Those are the kinds of questions you should ask the advisors at your target college and the community college.

Transferring to a Four-year College

At this point, you need to decide if you have the education you need to proceed with your calling or if you need to move on to a four-year college to finish preparing for your career. You may also need to start thinking about a master's degree or even a doctoral degree. If you need at least a bachelor's degree, you'll transfer to a four-year college. As when you first came out of high school, the choices are exhausting. The nice thing about this stage of life is that you now have some life experience and have taken two years of classes at the community college. You have gained additional maturity by living through those years. Your decision now should be much easier because you'll have a better grasp of your calling and how you need to prepare.

Now financing can become difficult. In upcoming chapters, we'll discuss paying for your additional years of college. Here I must repeat the caution: don't take the "easy" way out by signing up for a student loan. Keep in mind that you must repay every penny. For most people, the payments never seem to end. Many will take jobs that offer loan forgiveness. Others may find ways to eliminate the loans. Later, we'll discuss the impact of those student loans, along with ways to pay them down if you already have them.

Graduate School

There isn't much to add about graduate school (master's or doctoral degrees). Each step will require reevaluation of your life direction. You'll need to find out what educational and certification requirements you'll need. At the risk of sounding redundant, avoid student loans. They will be a future weight around your neck, keeping you from your calling and restricting your future choices.

One thing to consider before going into graduate school is a gap year (or more). In a recent podcast, John Stonestreet of the Colson Center noted that advice from Dr. Norman Geisler altered his direction in life just as he was ready to charge into graduate school (seminary). Dr. Geisler said, "Look, you've been in school now for 16 straight years, from basically kindergarten through graduating college. Take a year off. Go do something before going to seminary. And it was interesting how many of us actually took his advice. I did, and I'm really glad that I did, that I didn't jump right out of college into seminary. And there were things that happened in that year in between that just proved Dr. Geisler's advice to be really wise."[18]

If I had gone right into graduate school after earning my bachelor's degree, I would not have appreciated what I learned in the program. Building upon real-life experience made the master's degree more valuable.

When choosing a graduate program, consider both what you're already doing and what you think you want to do in the future. That way, you can determine what kind of graduate degree will be helpful. This decision is usually easier for people who are already involved in a profession.

Working—and working with others—can often help a person to determine where to go next. Many people work in an area of strength for a while and then decide to change. It's not uncommon for a technical person to wind up in management and desire an MBA. It's also not uncommon for someone to decide to work in a more people-oriented career, like counseling or ministry. While it takes a little more work to change careers entirely, you can probably find many programs to help you do so. When you enter a graduate program, be sure you don't take on debt, which would prohibit you from practicing what you are striving to learn.

FOUR

Paying for Your Education

How do you plan to pay for your education? We've covered some great ways to minimize the cost. Regrettably, few people can get an education for free.

Hudson Taylor, a Protestant missionary to China, said, "God's work done in God's way will never lack God's supply."[19] That was true in his time, and it's still true today. If God's plan for you includes college, the provision is there. The challenge is to find out specifically where the supply is and how to reach out and obtain it.

Regrettably, I have heard current students thank God for their school loans. They said there was no way they could have gone to college without school loans. I wonder if that's true. Do we believe God is no longer capable of providing for His work? I think God is still capable of providing, and I have seen Him do so. He is not some distant deity who created everything and left the rest to us. He cares about us and will provide for us.

I also wonder about those who thanked God for their student loans. They are surely now out of college and probably making payments on their debts. Do they continue to thank God for their still-outstanding debt and the ever-present payments? I received this comment from a graduate of a Christian university who had aimed to do international charity work, "It's pretty upsetting to both of us that no one discouraged us from taking out so much in loans, particularly from a school that claims to be focused on the

Great Commission."[20] This couple can't do what they felt called to do because of their large student-debt payments.

Varieties and Combinations of Methods to Pay for School

Through years of teaching God's principles for handling money, I have seen that God's usual provision for His people is through His people. I remember one specific person who could have fallen into the "no way to go to school without a loan" group. However, he prayed about it, and God provided through a lady at his church who had some extra money. She could think of nothing better to do with it than to help some deserving young man go to college. The moral of this story is that we should go to God first. You might have to wait, but God can provide. As my mentor used to say, "God is never late, but He is rarely early." God wants us to trust Him for our provision. But sometimes we have to wait.

Are other traditional sources of college funding wrong? Of course not. God could have simply made money appear in the poor widow's cupboard in Elijah's time (1 Kings 17). However, He used a small pot of oil to provide an abundance of oil, which the widow then sold. God is also not limited to using only "Christian" sources. Proverbs 13:22 tells us a sinner's wealth is stored up for the righteous. Scholarships, grants, and other sources of legitimate funding would be good ways to pay for your education.

There are many more ways of paying for an education than I could list here. They can also change very quickly. As a result, I'll discuss current major ways of paying for college, particularly those that don't involve debt. You might need to learn new ways of thinking and living, but they'll have lifelong value in your personal life, your social life, and your work life.

I would be neglectful if I didn't again emphasize prayer. God

21

wants us to seek Him to supply His direction for us and His provision for our needs. We seek God's direction through time spent with Him in prayer. In the appendix, I've listed some scriptures about God's provision and guidance. Your pastor or another spiritually mature person can recommend books on effective prayer. These resources will take you far beyond your college education and provide strength when your faith is challenged during your college career and beyond. And don't think your faith won't be challenged. It will, even if you go to a Christian college or university.

Scholarships and Grants

Scholarships and grants are usually considered free money. Most require an application process, and some of those processes are complicated, including essays on assigned topics. Scholarships and grants are a huge topic, so be prepared to do research on your own.

Economist, public commentator, and author Ben Kaplan has great information on going to college almost debt free. He says, "You'll discover that you're eligible for more scholarships than you probably think if you seek out scholarships from corporations, foundations, community organizations, and professional associations (in addition to those from individual colleges and the government)."[21] He recommends applying for everything that might remotely be available for you. The time spent applying can pay big dividends.

Many schools offer internal scholarships. A friend told me his boys got scholarships from their university for singing in the choir. And they weren't even music majors. He did add that they could both carry a tune.

As you apply, find out where the money is coming from. You don't want money from questionable sources. As God told us in

Proverbs 13:11, dishonest money dwindles away. You don't want to accept money from a questionable source and have it disappear after you're already locked into classes and have no other options. Questionable funding could be from businesses that make money through ungodly activities or through government lotteries, which are usually funded on the backs of those who can least afford it. This area requires prayer, discernment, and godly counsel.

Company Tuition Programs

Many companies in the US have tuition reimbursement or tuition payment programs. The June, 2017, issue of *Inc. Magazine* contained a list of the fifty best workplaces in the country.[22] Almost half offered tuition reimbursement programs. In an *Inc. Magazine* survey of Inc. 500 founders, 44 percent indicated their company had stipends for education.[23] Probably the most common programs reimburse full-time employees for taking college-level classes related to their job with the company. A good portion of my education was reimbursed by companies for which I worked. Some companies will also provide tuition reimbursement for part-time employees.

Tuition reimbursement sometimes includes books, supplies, and mileage to and from classes. Typically, employees take reimbursable classes outside work hours (either on campus or online), with the stipulation that the employee doesn't use work hours for studying or class. Rules and benefits of tuition reimbursement programs vary greatly. The human resources department can give you information.

The Bible tells us "when a man's ways please the Lord, he makes even his enemies to be at peace with him" (Proverbs 16:7, ESV). I have known of good employees, well liked by management, who were reimbursed for college classes that didn't relate at all to their jobs. Keep in mind that God is the one providing for this education. He can do that through a variety of sources.

Recently, some large companies have created programs that can take a part-time employee through a bachelor's degree at no cost. At the time of this writing, the list of companies offering this program included Chick-fil-A, McDonald's, Starbucks, and others. The programs often have interesting quirks but are worth investigating.

The Starbucks program pays for employees to get select degrees through a specific college via online classes.[24] For some, this is a wonderful opportunity. However, for others, online classes can be a disaster. As a primarily online instructor, I have worked with students who didn't have the self-motivation to succeed in this setting. For those students, the offer from Starbucks would lead to frustration and unmet expectations. It's important for you to understand your personality and giftings.

Personal Savings

At the beginning of this chapter, we discussed the need for patience when seeking to fund an education. In addition to patience, prospective students also need to learn to delay gratification. In other words, you don't get everything now and may need to wait for what you want. This mindset has always been unpopular as it goes against our selfish nature. But it's still as effective as it was in ancient times. In the appendix, you'll find Bible verses about patience and delayed gratification. If you are not operating from a Christian biblical perspective, I'm sure you can find similar advice within your religion or philosophy.

Personal savings is a great way to pay for schooling. It's not common for a new high school graduate to have significant money in savings, but here's where patience can pay off. If you're still in high school, move saving to the top of your to-do list. Often, relatives are happy to contribute to future schooling when birthdays, Christmas, and graduation come around. Put those gifts into savings, and you can reap interest. The earlier you start, the better. A good place to invest those gifts might be a 529 plan. We'll discuss 529 plans later in this chapter.

If you are close to graduation or have already graduated, taking a gap year to work might be wise. The gap year allows the student to mature and gives him time to work and earn some of his college money. During the gap year, a future student may even change her mind about her vocation. It's much cheaper to change direction in a gap year than during your college program.

The gap-year job can help pay for school, but you'll probably cobble together your college bill from a variety of sources. In the best-case scenario, this won't include debt.

The gap-year concept means different things to different people. Search "gap year" on the web, and most of your results will be programs in which a high school graduate travels during the year between high school and college. These programs are pricey, and if you travel during a gap year, you'll lose twelve to fourteen months of income otherwise put toward college expenses. If money is not available for college, it probably isn't available for a gap-year travel program.

Investigate the cost of gap-year travel. I found an "economical" option that cost $5,000 to $10,000. For most students, money spent on a gap year is money no longer available to spend on college, and they have to borrow funding for either or both. If you have a private student loan, the interest starts accumulating the day the money is issued to you or your college. At a rate of 4.5 percent (a good available rate for a student loan), using $7,500 of school loan money for an inexpensive gap-year trip could easily cost you just under $12,000. I calculated this using the average time most people pay on their bachelor's degree student loan: twenty-one years.[25]

Interest on Loans

For some, the concept of interest may be new. Without getting into the weeks of teaching that is required in college finance classes, you should understand that when people loan money, they expect to be paid back the money that was loaned. In addition, they expect to be paid extra by the borrower for the use of their money. This is called interest. College loans typically take many years to pay off. During those years, the lender is charging interest for the continued use of their money. This is why you may borrow $7,500 and wind up actually paying $12,000.

How the $18,000 was calculated

The $18,000 was estimated using a minimum wage of $11 per hour working full-time for 14 months between high school graduation and starting at your chosen school ($25,500 gross earnings less statutory payroll taxes). The net number will vary depending specific circumstances and in which state the student is employed.

During your gap-year trip, you also miss an entire year of income from a full-time job. Add the missed income of $18,000 (which would have reduced the need for part of a student loan) to the $7,500 cost of the gap-year trip, and you have to borrow or generate an extra $25,500.

After you make the twenty-one years of payments, the gap-year cost could approach a total of $40,000. That's 40 percent of the cost of going to a four-year state college. It could pay for even more of your schooling if you go to community college first and then transfer to the four-year college.

Some potential gap-year participants will moan that this is their only opportunity to travel and see the world. My response: "Baloney." We serve a big God, and He can provide for His people to go traveling and "see the world." Even if

26

you don't serve God in mission work, you can travel after college graduation. Traveling is more fun when it's already paid for. It's not as much fun when you know you'll come home to a large, difficult-to-pay-off credit-card bill. You get the freedom to relax and not worry about money if the money's already in the bank, waiting to be spent.

I don't believe there are "this is my only chance" situations in God's providence. God can provide for future trips without debt. For the average person in their gap year, traveling involves going into debt. Having missed the opportunity for earnings during that gap year puts the student even further into college debt. That kind of gap year is probably not a good idea for most high school graduates.

Parental or Other Family Support

Many forward-thinking parents and grandparents put aside money to help their children or grandchildren through college or other post-secondary schooling. Squeezing money to save from an average budget can be difficult but not impossible while raising a family. But diligent teens, parents, and grandparents can save for future schooling, and here's how.

A 2019 estimate for annual college fees shows an average cost of a four-year bachelor's degree, with the student living on campus, to be a little over $100,000 at a public not-for-profit college. The same calculation for a private not-for-profit college comes to $341,000. Private for-profit colleges run a little less at $250,000.[26] These figures do not take future inflation into consideration. On the other hand, if parents invest in a child's college costs by opening an investment account, inflation can be their friend. Especially if they have a tax-deferred account like a 529 plan.

A 529 plan is a special tax-deferred plan allowing college savings to grow with no tax penalty as the money grows. Exercise care in this process. Many 529 plans have significant fees that offset the tax benefits. One of the initial benefits for a properly configured 529 plan is that the contributions may be tax-deductible to the person or persons contributing to the plan, especially if the plan is in your state. To determine tax deductibility, consult a tax advisor. Assuming all the money is used for a qualifying educational expense, the money will come out of the plan tax-free.

Another benefit of the 529 plan is its transferability. If you are brilliant and receive a full-ride scholarship, your parents or grandparents could transfer your college money to another sibling, cousin, or whomever. With careful planning, the money will not be lost or heavily taxed.

Based on the estimated costs above, if parents start setting aside money for a child's four-year college costs at a public not-for-profit college in a tax-deferred plan when the child is born, they can get away with setting aside only $167 per month. If parents start setting aside money for the child's four-year college costs at a private not-for-profit college when the child is born, they will have to set aside $568 per month. If a parent starts setting aside money for the child's four-year college costs at a private for-profit college when the child is born, they will have to set aside $416 per month. These calculations assume the plan earns an annual 10 percent, compounded.

Wow! Those numbers are scary. If the parent does not use a tax-deferred plan, the numbers are even scarier, since taxes chip away at the earnings as the money grows. Providentially, most students don't need to pay the full tuition, room, board, books, etc. In later chapters, we'll discuss other funding methods that could reduce the raw dollars needed to get completely through a four-year degree or maybe beyond.

You can find internet calculators to give you an idea of the amount to set aside if you have special circumstances, such as shorter times in which to save, lower overall costs, higher overall costs, etc. Your calculations will be much more accurate if you know what college you wish to target and that school's estimated costs. And don't forget—if you spend your first two years at a community college, you need to come up with money for only two years of the much more expensive four-year college or university.

If parents or grandparents have not set aside any money for a child's college costs, they have other alternatives. The first is to provide help from the parents' or grandparents' current cash flow. Keep in mind that with a child moved out of the house, some of the regular household expenses are reduced. Those reductions will probably not be substantial, but in putting together a plan to fund a debt-free college career, every little bit helps.

Parents or grandparents could also choose to cut back on their expenditures to help the child get through college. One warning here is that parents should not give priority to paying their child's college costs over saving for a reasonable retirement. Social Security was never designed to provide a full retirement. Having money in the bank or a stream of income from another source on top of Social Security is the only way to have a reasonable retirement. Parents or grandparents should not bankrupt themselves to help a child get through college.

Earning College Credit Before College Enrollment

Depending on your academic status in high school and the flexibility of your school, you could enroll for college credit while still in high school. There are many common ways to do this and probably many others of which I am unaware. One way is to take classes at your local community college while still in high school. Often these classes count as both college and high school credit. In some cases, you might have to pay extra fees to get the college credits.

When I was finishing high school, I was allowed to leave campus during my senior year and drive to the local state university for classes. I had to enroll, but I didn't have dorm or meal plans to pay for. So I started my full-time college career with a collection of inexpensive college credits that had none of the extra costs of full-time college enrollment.

In the online learning environment where I teach, I have often had high school students in undergraduate classes, enrolled for dual credit. They earned credits to finish high school and also credits as a head start for their college careers. The same benefits of going to the college campus during high school would apply, except you'd have no costs for driving to school or parking.

Before embarking on a dual-credit or early college classes program, be sure your college of choice will accept those credits. There should be no problem, but it's always safe to check ahead of time. And if possible, get the determination in writing.

In many cases, opportunities to take Advanced Placement (AP) classes and tests before you start college can allow you to skip some lower-division general education classes. According to the college board, "nearly all colleges and universities in the United States grant credit and placement for qualifying AP scores."[27] AP classes are not easy ways to get credits and will require significant extra work. But the student can save time and money by using this option. The classes are to prepare for the tests, but the classes aren't required before taking the tests.

There are fees for the tests and the classes. Also, there are timing issues, as the exams are not offered year round. However, the exams cost a small fraction of the price of taking the classes. And the topics available in AP classes are limited. For best use of this tool, the process should start before the end of your junior year in high school.

Support from Your Spouse

Many couples help each other get through college. My wife has three PHT (Putting Him Through) degrees. Not only did she help provide the money to pay for the schooling, but she also supported me through the process. It's not uncommon for one spouse to work while the other goes to college. Often, spouses agree that, when the first graduates, the other will go to college, supported by the new graduate and his or her increased earning power. Since my wife had already finished her bachelor's degree before we got married, I didn't get the opportunity to earn my PHT (Putting Her Through). I'm just one blessed and thankful husband.

As with previous methods of support, this involves sacrifice. Used cars, appliances, electronics, etc. usually run as well as new items. They aren't as slick and maybe the resolution on an older TV isn't as good the new HDTVs, but the goal is a college degree. After that, you can improve your lifestyle . . . or maybe not, if you have goals beyond the degree. Sometimes it's important to defer gratification.

Deferred gratification is when you decide something in the future is more important than the thing you want now. A good example of this might be a new car. Your old car may be annoying with squeaks, rattles, and an eyesore paint job. But it runs great and is dependable. You desire a new car, or at least a newer car. The principle of needs and wants comes into play here. You don't need a newer car, but you want one, maybe in the worst way. However, you also have a goal of completing college and earning enough money to support your family and give of your time and money to help a special ministry or mission. In light of eternity, which is more important, a college degree or a new car? And don't consider financing the new car. Debt is debt, and any debt will drag you down.

Deferred gratification can be a real downer. It's not easy to say no to things that sound like great ideas. When you get discouraged, keep in mind the statistic about earning power with a college degree, referenced at the beginning of chapter two. And keep in mind the freedom you will have in the future with no college debt and a good income based upon a college degree.

Friends and Others

Richard Foster's meetings of clearness, discussed in chapter two, can clarify your direction and be a "catalyst for ministry and provide a basis for emotional and even financial support."[28] The typical plea for support revolves around doing ministry, mission, or humanitarian effort. But it's not uncommon, in this age of funding pleas on the internet, to find people asking for help to get through college. While that may not be the best way to get your college support, something along those lines could help.

There are myriad ways to do funding on the internet, and I won't try to cover them all. But the place to start is with family and friends. In my experience, God's typical way to care for His people is through His people. If you feel this is a way to help find funding, you will need to create a way to explain the need to those whom you will ask. Funding requests don't have to be formal. You're not trying to get millions to start a new company. But you will need to state the vision for your life, including your education, in a short and succinct manner, and explain why your degree program deserves support.

As with all the ways of finding the funds to get through college, you should pray about this and seek counsel. Keep in mind that if you don't ask, you are making someone's decision for them. Also, remember the worst that can happen is they will say no. A friend of mine who was a professional fund-raiser told me that most often, the negative answers were courteously given and usually with regret that the potential donor couldn't help at that time. Hearing a "no" answer doesn't have to be painful or embarrassing.

Military

Another way to pay for college is by signing up for the military before enrolling. Our military needs college-educated personnel to provide leadership and to operate the extremely complicated systems used to avoid or wage war. To recruit college-educated personnel, the various branches of our military are willing to provide scholarships, books, and monthly stipends to those who agree to work as officers in their service branch for a specified number of years. The following quotes are from the ROTC websites of the Army, the Air Force, and the Navy.

* Scholarships and stipends in Army ROTC pay for college courses and help you focus on what's important. Namely, getting that college degree—not how you'll pay for it.[29]

* In AFROTC, you'll not only build lifelong friendships, but you may also have the opportunity to pay for college through our scholarship programs.[30]

* Selected applicants for the Navy ROTC Scholarship Program are awarded scholarships through a highly competitive national selection process, and receive full tuition, books stipend, educational fees, and other financial benefits at many of the country's leading colleges and universities. Upon graduation, midshipmen are commissioned as officers in the unrestricted line Naval Reserve or Marine Corps Reserve.[31]

There are many benefits to this way of paying for an education, and there are some drawbacks. The benefits include graduating from college with no student debt, leadership training from some of the best-led organizations in the world, an appointment as a military officer already lined up when you graduate, inclusion in community projects during your schooling, inclusion in the US GI Bill, and the opportunity to serve your country.

The most obvious drawback is that, to avail yourself of these scholarships and other support, you need to commit to time spent in the branch of service you select. Currently, to get full financial support through a four-year degree, you must commit to three years of active service plus five years of service in the reserves or up to five years of active service. Be sure to check out the details with the branch of service you are considering. There is also a risk of spending time in a place where people shoot at you. Or you might be assigned to an unpleasant location. But remember that God cares about you and can bring you through any difficulty. The safest place for us to live is the middle of God's plan for us. If God's plan for you is the military, it's the safest place for you.

The US military needs trained personnel of all types. You can pursue engineering, accounting, personnel, medicine, law, and more. On the ROTC program, you can attend a secular college or a religious school. You don't need to sign away your faith to go into the Armed Forces in the United States.

The US Coast Guard has a program alongside the Army, the Navy (including the Marines), and the Air Force. I will cover this option in chapter eight, as it appears to be primarily a degree-completion program after your first year or two of college. Also, be aware of the strict age requirements for these programs.

Military Academies

Along with the ROTC program, most branches of the US military also have Military Academies. The Merchant Marine also has an academy. Competition for appointments into these academies is fierce. For most students, the nomination process leads through their US senators, their US congressional representative, or the vice president of the United States. There are exceptions, but they won't apply to most of us. Each of these nominators is allowed to have only a certain number of students in any academy at a time. That's partially why the nomination process is so competitive.

For the 2017 school year, the Air Force Academy received more than 12,000 applications. Of those 12,000, only 2,277 were qualified. Of those, the academy made only 1,475 offers of admission. The total number admitted was 1,190.[32] Less than 10 percent of applicants managed to get an appointment and enroll.

Each academy requires a commitment to service upon graduation. For example, an Air Force Academy graduate must accept an appointment and serve as a commissioned officer for at least eight years after graduation. Five of those years must be active duty and the remainder served as inactive reserve. The benefits and drawbacks listed in the prior section apply. But here we have one additional benefit. The military academies in this country are recognized as some of the top colleges in the world. Remember chapter three, where I said employers don't care where you earned your degree? Military academies are the exception. Having a military academy degree on your resume can open doors to places a degree from other schools might not.

GI Bill

If you are finishing your time in the military or still on active duty, you may be eligible for GI Bill benefits to help pay for your schooling. Carefully managed, these can get you through a four-year degree and maybe even beyond. "The Post-9/11 GI Bill provides education benefits for those who have served on active duty for 90 or more days after Sept. 10, 2001."[33] The amount of benefits depends on how much time you spent on active duty beyond a ninety-day minimum. It also requires an honorable discharge if you are out of the service. Service-connected disability discharges have a different set of rules.

The Post-9/11 GI Bill can pay up to 100 percent of tuition and fees, a monthly housing allowance, and a generous amount for books and supplies. Reserves and the National Guard have different rules, but you may still qualify. As with most government programs, it's complicated. Additionally, they offer opportunities to transfer benefits to a spouse or children. Again, the rules are complicated, but it's worth investigating.

You can use these benefits to go to college, university, vocational school, technical school, apprenticeship programs, and much more. Since the list might change the day after publication of this book, you'll need to investigate further to find out the benefits available for someone in your circumstances. The military has other programs besides the Post-9/11 GI Bill. They include the Montgomery GI Bill[34] and the Reserve and Guard GI Bill.[35] Both of these have like benefits but different rules and qualifications. All are worth investigating. You might find a way to get a debt-free degree.

If you have a VA disability and an employment handicap (both defined by the program rules), you might qualify for extra benefits, including counseling, rehabilitation, job placement services, and other services.[36] You can get information at your VA office or hospital. If you have served your country, I thank you. I also hope you will accept the thanks of your country and use the benefits offered to you for further education or training.

Work-for-Tuition Programs

A number of colleges advertise work-for-tuition programs. Some even offer work-for-all-costs programs. Remember that tuition is not the only cost of going to college, but it certainly is a big chunk of the total price. Room, board, and books can easily add up to $13,000 a year. For these programs, students may be required to work during the semester (ten to twenty hours per week, depending on the school). Some schools require all students to

Private Not-For-Profit Colleges:	
Room and Board	$12,000
Books & Costs	1,000
Total	$13,000

work, sometimes on campus and sometimes in community service. At least one school has a farm where the students work.[37] Since most of these colleges are smaller schools, competition for the tuition-free slots is fierce. An excellent high school GPA and high SAT scores can help you gain admission to your program of interest. The school may also have other requirements, such as living in a certain area of the country, being a full-time student, living on campus, or being in a certain age group. At least one technical school with free tuition accepts only students who are unmarried and under twenty-one.

Interestingly, many Ivy-League schools also offer free tuition for qualified students who can prove financial need. The list as of this writing includes Cornell University, Duke University, Harvard University, Massachusetts Institute of Technology, Princeton University, Stanford University, Texas A&M University, the

University of North Carolina at Chapel Hill, Vanderbilt University, and Yale University. With the current pressure on colleges to hold down students' costs, there may be others as well. The tuition is typically based on a sliding scale, considering the parents' income and other factors. As I said earlier, if you are rich or poor, paying can be a non-issue. If you are in the middle like most of us, it's a huge issue.

Work-study Programs

"Work-study is a federally and sometimes state-funded program that helps college students with financial need to get part-time jobs."[38] Work-study will not cover all college costs. However, it can be a piece of the package and could allow you to graduate from college debt free. Applying to a work-study program is the same as applying for student financial aid. As of this writing, over 3,000 colleges and universities participate in the program.

A benefit of the work-study program for the college is that the state or federal government may pay up to 50 percent of the wages earned through the program. In essence, the college could wind up with half-price employees. There are restrictions for the applicant, relating to a lack of ability to pay for college, and there are restrictions for the college, relating to the ways the provided government funding is used. The big benefit for students is that they don't have to borrow and repay this money. You can find details on a program like this through a college's financial-aid office.

Work

Working your way through college is a common way to get a degree. Studies have shown that students who work while going to college are typically better performers in the classroom and get better grades. "The Bureau of Labor Statistics found that students who worked less than 20 hours per week had an average GPA of 3.13, while nonworking students had an average GPA of 3.04."[39] Research also shows that students working fulltime and going to school fulltime do not do as well. With the current cost of college, part-time work would again be just a piece of the financial puzzle. But every dollar earned along the way (if wisely spent) will reduce or help to eliminate the debt burden upon graduation.

College is not supposed to be a place to play a lot and maybe learn a little, as it's often portrayed in popular films and TV shows. Keeping time free at college to party or hang out with friends sounds nice, but the long-term cost of doing so has resulted in many derailed life plans and a burden of debt. This can crush graduates, their marriages, and their families.

Some have been forced to delay marriage or postpone starting a family to pay off student debt.[40] Also, "debt can bring big problems to your marriage. Nearly 80 percent of the couples who get a divorce cite financial difficulties as one of the major reasons, according to *The Dollar Stretcher*."[41] This same article stated, "With debt hanging over your head, you're not able to save for other things, like a comfortable retirement, nice things for your children, or even a trip to the Bahamas." Is that the way you want to enter what should be the best relationship of your life?

While paying as you go sounds like an impossible task, a physician friend of mine started a lawn-care business in college. This helped pay his way through medical school. After he graduated, he sold his lawn-care route. He was not only debt-free, but he also had money in his pocket. He is still quite frugal. You may not be as entrepreneurial as this, but you can find plenty of jobs beyond just delivering pizza or making lattes.

Another benefit of working during college is that many companies will help pay for your college, above and beyond your salary. Companies in this country realize the burden of college debt and the impact excessive college debt has on their current and future employees.

Summer Jobs

Summer jobs can help as well. During the school year, it's not a good idea to work fulltime, since it can cause class performance to drop. However, in the summer, full-time work is not only possible but also a good idea.

Finding a job related to your targeted future career would be wonderful. But it's more likely that the summer job will be minimum-wage work in a field in which jobs are available. Don't look down on a minimum-wage job. All honest work is honorable if done with excellence. It'll also look good on your future resume. Your potential employer will see that you have already developed good work habits.

One UConn professor wrote an article telling what students should do during the summer.[42] His short list included relaxing, catching up with family and friends, taking a summer course, taking on a summer job, and traveling. Oh, that every college student had the luxury to do the first, second, and fifth. If avoiding college debt is your goal, those three activities are nice but must be tempered with the determination that being debt-free is a more important goal.

Summer classes can be a good choice, and we'll discuss them in the next chapter. But the most productive choice is probably going to be work. A quick web search can give you ideas for jobs ideal for college students on summer break. Cull these lists according to your aptitude, skills, and interests. You'll also need to weed out inappropriate jobs and jobs in locations where the cost of living is high.

Good jobs include things like lifeguard, camp counselor, landscaper, sign holder, server, busser, housekeeper, nanny, private tutor, pet sitter, dog walker, bookstore sales associate, retail sales associate, parking attendant, food delivery driver, hotel desk agent, paid political activist, park (national, state, etc.) employee, tour guide, community center worker, and many more. Pay varies depending on the skills required, the type of job, your experience, and the location. Keep in mind that jobs paying more due to location typically come with a higher cost of living. You could easily net much less for a high-paying job if you spend most of your take-home pay on living expenses.

Once again, your goal is to use the money for college costs. Open a savings account and put all but what you need for daily living into that account. Don't have checks for that account. Put the debit card in a safe but not easily accessible spot. You don't want to spend your summer earnings on something impulsive. If impulses are an issue for you, be sure to look at the Impulse List section in chapter nine.

Loans

The Department of Education offers some excellent comments on student loans. The beginning paragraph of the federal student aid website says, "If you apply for financial aid, you may be offered loans as part of your college's financial aid offer. A loan is money you borrow and must pay back with interest."[43] The last sentence in this quote is the crux of the issue, and it is why this section on loans is the last section in the chapter. Borrowing should be your last option for paying for your college or technical school.

As I said earlier, God can provide for your education without a loan. I have seen it happen. It happened to me, and I believe it can happen again. I believe that God's best for His people is to stay out of the bondage of debt. That said, we still need to discuss the issue of borrowing. Once again, this is a very complex area, so I will cover only the essentials here.

Basically, two types of loans are used to fund educational costs: federal loans and private loans. Should you decide to borrow money, it's best to get a federal loan first. The biggest benefits of a federal loan (as opposed to a private loan) are fixed interest rates, deferred interest accrual, and income-driven repayment plans.[44] These three benefits alone can save significant money and significant anxiety. One additional benefit of a federal loan is the possibility of loan principal forgiveness if you are willing to work in public service or other specified vocations, or if you qualify for an income-driven payment plan. I'll cover loan principal forgiveness in more detail in chapter eight.

Regrettably, deciding between federal or private borrowing is not your only decision if you take this option. There are different types of federal loans, including federal loans incurred by your parents to pay for your schooling. This is a good time to repeat the caution I gave earlier in this chapter: parents or grandparents should not bankrupt themselves to provide for a child's education.

The federal government offers two kinds of loans: direct subsidized loans and direct unsubsidized loans. The difference is basically the terms of the loan. Direct subsidized loans are available only to those who can demonstrate financial need. You'll need to investigate the advantages and disadvantages for your circumstances.

The federal government also offers the Direct PLUS loan.[45] Direct PLUS loans are good for both parents and students. However, they are probably the least desirable of the federal loan options. Put them toward the bottom of your option list.

Private student loans are just as they sound. An individual issues a loan to pay for the student's schooling. The terms of the loan depend upon the lender and the borrower's creditworthiness. If the student doesn't have any credit, the parents may need to cosign the loan. Pray long and hard before you agree to cosign a loan for anyone, including your children. In the Scripture Appendix, you'll find a list of scriptures related to cosigning. To say the least, God has severe warnings for those who would cosign a loan.

Private loans also include loans directly from the college. If you choose to accept one of these loans, be sure you understand the terms before you agree to the loan. It might be a good deal, or it might not.

Remember, the whole point of this book is to help a student and his or her parents to see that doing the easy thing (taking out student loans) is rarely the best way to pay for college. Regrettably, I know of people who have gone the easy way and were unable to follow the calling on their lives. This includes becoming a missionary or pastor or entering a fulfilling field that typically does not pay well.

The wisdom of staying out of debt applies to any borrowing, not just college loans. The stress of payments, particularly long-term and large ones, has destroyed many a marriage. Money is not always the reason for the relationship's failure. But the stress of making payments adds to other marital stresses they probably could have handled if they didn't have the money stress. We'll discuss ways to pay off existing student loans in chapters nine and ten.

FIVE

Stretching Resources During College

Regrettably, many college students have received little or no instruction on managing money. Therefore, they don't look at long-term consequences and so they fall into many money-handling errors. In this chapter, we'll cover ways to make your money stretch further. In the next chapter I'll cover some common things college students do that result in increasing student debt or spending money they could have used to avoid student debt. Most of these relate to on-campus students. Many also relate to online students.

Negotiating with Your College
After You've Been Accepted

"Research shows that applicants who commit to one college early tend to get less aid money than those who wait and end up with acceptance offers from several colleges. That's especially true for applicants vying for merit scholarships, which usually go to students a college is trying to lure away from a competitor."[46]

The first step is not to accept the offer right away. On the other hand, be sure not to let the deadline or the offer from the college expire unless you have decided against that college. Keep your options open as long as you can.

As the application deadline approaches, contact your top-choice college and request more scholarship money. Look for reasons for your college to give you more money. Be polite about it, but ask your recruiter about potential unclaimed scholarships or other available non-loan money.

Be honest and explain that their school is your top choice, but you need more scholarship money, or you can't attend there. Be prepared to refuse to take out college loans at all, or at least limit the loans you will take. College finance officers can be like car salespeople offering car loans. A quick fallback position for the college is to offer more student loans. That's not what you want.

Assuming you have an acceptance letter in front of you and they say "no" to more scholarships or grants, you are still in a position to attend that college and figure out another way to finance it. Keep in mind that God sometimes guides people through not providing as well as through providing. God may not want you to attend there, and the lack of provision may be His way of telling you.

Course Planning

Through smart planning and course selection, it's possible to reduce the amount of time you'll spend at your chosen college. Concentrate on the required courses for your major. They will include required general-education classes. Even though your friends may take fun classes, remember the class costs money.

If you feel you must join that class with your friends, you might have the option of

Auditing a class

Auditing a class is attending and participating in a class, but not getting academic credit for the class. It is an enrichment activity allowing you to learn what the class teaches. To audit the class, you first need permission. There still may be a charge, but it is usually much less than regular tuition. Part of auditing also involves showing up for class, participating in discussion when the professor indicates that it is OK, and doing all other class activities as directed by the professor.

auditing it. Auditing is a way to participate without paying full tuition for the class. If you audit a class, you will not earn academic credit for it, but you can participate in the learning value or the opportunity to spend time with friends. Be sure your commitment of time and effort is worth the auditing. If you think the class is important, maybe you should register for it, earn the credit, and participate fully in the class. It could fit into the elective requirements in your degree program.

We've discussed the cost of changing majors during your college career, but we need to be realistic. Many students go to college straight out of high school and have no idea what they want to do with their lives, even after doing personality and vocational testing. For these students, changing majors is cheaper and much less painful than changing careers years later. Change your major if you need to, despite the extra cost, since your degree may determine your course in life for the next forty years. You still want to do your best to keep the costs down. But sometimes things have to change, and you need to take a more expensive route. God is capable of providing for that too.

Taking Challenge Tests

Some colleges and universities recognize that students entering their school may already have a certain skill and that sitting through a class in that area would be a waste of time, effort, and money. Students can sometimes test out of certain classes and still get the credit. Often, the student challenging the class takes the final exam. A challenge requires the approval of the instructor of the class and, often, the dean of the school. There is usually a fee, but it's often much less than the regular tuition for the class.

If you have a hobby or special interest in which you can take a class, you might be able to take a challenge test and save the cost of the class. There are restrictions and rules, but this is another way to make your money stretch and avoid borrowing.

Summer School or Online Substitute Classes

Another option is taking summer classes or online classes through another school. Often, these classes are less expensive. Summer and online classes allow you to pack more learning into your time at college and could allow you to graduate significantly early. For every semester you are not at college, you rack up fewer fees and costs.

However, I would offer three points of warning. First, summer may be a better time for you to return home and take a job to earn money to help pay for your continued education. At home, you typically do not have to pay for food and lodging, and you can use the money you earned to pay college expenses in the following semesters.

Also, try not to schedule too many classes. I teach college online, and I've had many students who struggled through their class because their class load was too heavy. You want to get through college and earn your degree, but you also want to do it with excellence. A too-heavy academic load will hinder excellence.

You also need to be sure the class you are taking will be accepted as part of your degree program. Ask if transferring college credits from an online college or university will be a problem.

Using Available Tax Credits

Another way to make your money stretch is to claim available tax credits when you file your income tax. Tax credits are available for tuition, fees, and course materials. To get those tax credits, you must pay the costs from an ordinary checking, savings, or taxable investment account.[47] In other words, if you are paying your tuition and fees out of a 529 account (discussed in chapter four), you are not eligible for the tax credit. Interestingly, many taxpayers receive tax-credit payments even if they didn't earn any income that year.

Buying Used Books

Books are a significant expense for a college student. During my college career, I made a point of going to the bookstore as soon as I knew what books I'd need for each of my classes. For most of the classes, I bought used books. Sure, it was annoying to have someone else's markings in the book and maybe have some torn pages. But it saved me a lot of money.

However, I made the mistake of not selling almost all my books as soon as the class was over. I kept only books related to my major, but I doubt I have ever reopened more than one or two of them. These days, you can find any information you need on the internet. The more books you can sell back, the less money you may have to borrow.

Investigating Alternative Housing

Living in college dorms can be a lot of fun. Many social activities revolve around the dorms, and you can make lifelong friendships there. However, you need to decide whether the cost of the dorms is worth those friendships and if you can make those friends in other ways. Dorm living can easily distract you from your academic progress. With all the social activity and the noise of so many people living in the same place, it can be difficult to study. If you have a detailed and complicated major, dorm life could be the death of your academic career. It could be so distracting that you'd need to retake a class in which you performed poorly. To save your academic career, you could find another place to study, like the college library or study areas.

That said, there are usually alternatives to living in a dorm. Some colleges, particularly religious ones, have rules mandating that first-year students and possibly higher-level students live in the dorms. If you have the freedom to live off campus, investigate the idea of renting an apartment with close friends or getting into a co-op housing situation.

While doing this investigation, keep in mind the extra costs of living in an apartment or a co-op housing situation. Include electricity and water for the apartment or co-op, which would not be charged in the dorm. If you live off campus, you might need to bring a car to college. We'll discuss having a car at college in the next chapter. Off-campus housing is a point worth looking at, but the dorm may still wind up being a better financial deal.

Remember, dorm costs go down when you have roommates. Or maybe I should say dorm costs go up when you decide not to have roommates. Investigate thoroughly before you make a decision. Try to find someone you like, who has similar career goals. You and your roommate could provide needed moral support to each other when things get busy and stressful.

Six

Common Errors To Avoid

Bringing a Car to College

There is an old saying that a boat is a hole in the water into which you pour money. Having owned a couple of small boats, I can attest to that. Cars are somewhat the same. Unless you absolutely need a car on campus (see the section in chapter four on needs and wants), you shouldn't have one. It's difficult to own a car, keep it insured and registered, and to do minimal upkeep maintenance for less than $600 or $700 per year. Routine car maintenance for a car in good shape should run around $100 a year.[48] Lest you think you can get by without maintaining your car, the endnote article also warns that deferring maintenance will end up costing you much more in the long run. If the car is of reasonable value, your annual registration should be under $100. The big-ticket item is insurance. Car insurance for those in their late teens and twenties can easily run $500 a year.

AAA estimates the annual cost of owning a car is over $6,000 a year.[49] That number probably includes payments. On top of that is gas. And if you're going to save money on gas by not using the car, why have the car there in the first place? Probably the final nail in the coffin of a college car is the cost of parking. Many colleges charge a parking fee. That fee will depend on the college.

A reasonable alternative is a bicycle. Bicycles don't require insurance, have minimal maintenance, and I don't know of any colleges charging fees for keeping a bicycle on campus. For longer trips or special occasions, students often share rides or use commercial rideshare or a taxi. The alternatives can save a lot of money very quickly.

Misusing Available Money

It's an all-too-common practice for students to use extra loan proceeds to buy electronics, dinners out, or other non-school items. While that's probably legal, it's not a great idea. As I discussed in chapter four, it's important to understand the difference between needs and wants. Do you really need a new TV or the latest cell phone? In light of your long-term plan or even eternity, is it a good idea?

Another side of an impulse purchase (which this kind usually is) is the total cost. If you have a private student loan, the interest started accumulating the day the money was issued to you or your college. At a rate of 4.5 percent (a good available rate for a student loan at this writing), using fifty dollars of your college loan for dinner out with your boyfriend or girlfriend could easily cost you over eighty dollars. The eighty dollars is calculated using the average of twenty-one years[50] after graduation to pay off the student loans for a bachelor's degree and your dinner out in your freshman year. It's amazing what a difference the small decisions make.

Taking a Semester Overseas

Semesters overseas are common. Even if you have the money in the bank to pay the extra fees, that money is better spent by avoiding loans for future semesters. Semesters overseas can be wonderful experiences. I have traveled overseas. It is an eye-opening and broadening experience. I highly recommend it. But not if you have to borrow for your trip.

Costs for study-abroad programs vary by college. Some colleges include the costs (including room and board) in their standard semester costs. Others cover only tuition for the program as part of the standard tuition, and all other costs are extra (transportation, room, and board). None of the programs I found included the incidentals of living in another country for several months. The estimate at one college was $1,000 per month for non-covered incidentals.[51] Colleges typically have program fees and require international health insurance. All those costs add up.

Adding significant cost to your college debt to go overseas is not a great idea. The same logic applies to a semester overseas and traveling during a gap year. Some potential semester-abroad participants think this is their only opportunity to travel and see the world. But we serve a big God, and He can provide for His people to travel and "see the world." I don't believe God's providence includes "this is my only chance" opportunities. God can provide for future trips, including those that don't put you into debt.

Taking a semester overseas using college debt is another way into bondage. Using the same logic as the dinner out in your freshman year, look at the long-term cost of an inexpensive study-abroad semester in your junior year. Figuring a minimal cost of $6,000 for the total incidentals, fees, and insurance, the semester abroad will cost over $9,600 by the time you pay off your loans.

You also miss an entire semester of income from your part-time job during that trip. Remember, working while in college not only typically results in better grades, but it also provides income you can use to support yourself without borrowing, or at least to borrow less. Including lost income in the equation, the cost of an inexpensive semester abroad can exceed a total cost of $14,000.

If you want to travel during your school time, consider joining the college choir, band, or a traveling sports team at the college. Most of the travel will be local or regional, but there are exceptions.

During my freshman year of college, our college choir traveled from California to New York, performing along the way. When we got to New York, we flew to England, then to Israel, then to Western Europe. We performed in many venues. When we got back to New York, we drove home to California, performing along the way. Using fundraisers to pay for individual costs, we spent money just for souvenirs and sundries on the trip. Sure, we lost a summer's potential income. But I still managed to graduate with my BA and no debt.

Meal Plans

If you live on campus, or even if you don't, consider passing on the full meal plan. There are often partial meal plans, including only a certain number of meals or excluding certain meals. You may not be a morning person and don't intend to have a full breakfast. Why pay for a full breakfast you aren't eating? Instead, you could make your breakfast a granola bar and a cup of coffee (or if you are like me, tea).

If you are anywhere near home or plan to visit friends on weekends, you may again be paying for food you are not eating. Think about your weekly college schedule. Don't forget that if you plan to keep food around to avoid paying for the full meal plan, you'll need time to shop now and then. You'll also need to be careful to discourage ants and other bugs in your living quarters, get a healthy diet, and buy groceries you can store and cook in your living arrangement. A healthy diet is important to keep your mind in good shape for your academics and for sufficient energy if you participate in athletics.

After your first year, reevaluate this decision. Avoid bringing a car so you can eat out. That's not likely to save money by the time you add the cost of having a car.

New Dorm Furniture

Dorm rooms usually have some basic furniture. Apartments may or not be furnished. Some colleges will suggest items to bring for their dorm rooms. Many families make the mistake of buying all new furniture and accessories for the dorm room or apartment.

Used furniture is fine. Used accessories are fine. Typically, the new student is not going to get an entirely new wardrobe, so why start with all new furniture and accessories? If nothing else, coordinate with roommates and decide who will bring which big-ticket item (a TV, a mini-fridge, etc.). Many colleges prohibit certain appliances in the dorm rooms, like hot plates, so be sure you know your college's rules.

Athletic Passes

If your college of choice has a lot of athletics, you will undoubtedly have the opportunity to buy a season pass. Think about it before you buy it. Will you go to all the games or only some of them? There may be opportunities to volunteer at the games, in which case you could see the game for free. If you are going to be in the band or cheer squad, you should get in free. These are not high costs, but with athletic passes sometimes going for over $140 per year,[52] the total cost by the end of your loan payments could exceed $200 for each annual pass.

School Health Insurance

If you are going to remain on your parents' health plan, don't sign up for school insurance too. Usually, the school health insurance is not expensive, but every dollar spent is a dollar that could increase a loan balance.

Eating Out

As you decide whether to buy the full meal plan, keep in mind that eating out is significantly more expensive than eating at the commons or cafeteria. And the cost of a date increases if you used borrowed money. The cost of eating out can inflate even faster if you use a credit card and don't pay it off every month. Credit card interest is significantly higher than most college loans. Don't add insult to injury by graduating with a large college loan and a large credit card balance. Better to limit meals out and control your spending by using a spending plan. I'll cover spending plans in detail in chapter nine.

Don't be afraid to use coupons and websites like restaurant.com to get discounts. There are many ways to save money at restaurants. If your date objects, you may have other issues to resolve beyond the cost of a meal.

Traveling To and From College

If you live a long distance from your college, travel could be a money issue. And there are more ways to travel than just airplanes. Depending on your college's location and where your family lives, you might be able to take a train or bus or even share a ride with friends. Taking the train or bus can be a lot less hassle than going through security at an airport, and it's cheaper. The train or bus can also give you time to decompress from the stress of studying and class deadlines. You can get home feeling more relaxed. Trains have wider seats and more space between the seats than airplanes do. On a train or bus, it's not a big hassle to get up, stretch, and use the restroom. While the bus may stop at a place for supposedly cheap meals, taking sandwiches and fruit can keep the overall cost down when traveling. Carrying snacks or food is also a way to save money on plane flights home and back.

Sharing a ride with friends can be a crazy but fun activity. Be sure to choose a good driver, and make sure the driver is not chemically impaired in any way (legal or illegal). Impaired driving is not acceptable on the road, even in states where recreational marijuana is legal. Also, before the trip starts, be sure everyone has agreed on sharing costs. Nothing will spoil a trip more than getting to the destination and arguing about how to divide the cost: the price of gasoline versus total per-mile costs (gasoline plus other costs of driving).

One more option is to stay at college during some of your breaks. Some of your college friends may live close and invite you to their homes. Don't ask to go home with a friend but leave the door open for an offer.

Think Twice about Parents' Weekends

Many colleges hold a parent weekend in the fall. They have special activities during the weekend, like a football game or some other athletic event. These are special times for parents to meet professors and other school personnel. They're well attended, which is great.

However, when hordes of parents descend upon a college town, prices go up. Some Iowa hotels, for example, charge more than double the usual nightly rate for the parent weekend.

Check with your college, but parents are usually welcome to visit almost any time. Parents are also welcome at athletic events. If I were going to select a weekend to visit a child at college, I would be more interested in hearing a concert or seeing a play at the college. I certainly would not be interested in paying double hotel room rates and being herded around with a mob of other parents. You can also avoid creating more debt by saving money here.

Concierge Services

Concierge services are optional services provided to make college life easier for a student. These could include errand services, picking up prescriptions, laundry service, etc. Some people think preventing distractions from the student's studies is worth the money. I think this is the time students need to learn to take care of themselves and balance full-time responsibilities.

People performing errand services in 2012 ran from $25–$40 an hour, and laundry service would run around $400 a year. The long-term cost of those expenditures, if added to college loans, would be much higher. Students should learn to do those things before going out into the world, and laundry, shopping, and other errands are a good place to start.

Fraternities or Sororities

Many successful people believe belonging to their fraternity or sorority changed their lives. Fraternity or sorority involvement generated life-long friendships and business connections, which have been good for them along the way. In 2012, fraternity costs ran from about $1,000 to $3,500 a year, and more for some. Throughout a four-year degree, that's $4,000 to $14,000 or more. Is the money available, and is the fraternity or sorority important enough to warrant this expenditure?

I would not say membership in a fraternity or sorority is not worth it. But students should consider the cost versus benefits before pledging. A student can look for scholarships for membership fees through the fraternity or sorority's national website. They can also rent tuxedos and gowns for formal occasions rather than buying those expensive items. They could borrow some of these items from friends or family.

Buying Insignia Items

Most students should not go crazy buying college apparel and accessories. If you want school logo attire and accessories, wait until after you graduate, have started a reasonable spending plan that includes loan payments, and have an income. To be frugal, you can visit thrift stores in your college town. You can also put logo or insignia items on your wishlist for a birthday or other gift-giving holiday. Grandparents and parents often look for mid-priced items to give to college-age children or grandchildren. Buying for a teenager or an early-twentysomething is not easy. Maybe the insignia item would make a perfect gift. Make it easier for them to give what you feel you need.

Buying logo apparel or accessories is not one of those things you have to do while at college. You can do this throughout your lifetime. Typically, you can afford to make those purchases later without taking on debt.

Seven

Ways To Continue Debt Free

Most of the content of chapters two through six applies to the rest of your college career. If you're in college and have a year or two paid for, you still need to figure out how to avoid debt for the rest of your college career. You might need to find more money. Things happen. The relative helping you might become ill or worse, and one or more of your sources might dry up. The organization that promised you money for all four years might have a bad year in the market and stop awarding money. You might slip up in a class and lose a scholarship because of a marginal grade.

Colleges often increase their charges to make ends meet, and you may now need more than you have cobbled together. While I was working on one of my degrees, the per-unit tuition increased by an average of 9 percent per year. One of those years, the increase was over 20 percent.

You should spend time on maintaining your chosen and successful manner of paying for your college career. Don't be complacent. Scholarships are available for students who have already started college. They're not as plentiful, but they're there. Keep up with the opportunities and be prepared to seek new funding sources if needed.

If you're at the end of your community college time and ready to move into a four-year college, costs will go up, and classes will get more difficult. Can you continue to work? Probably, but you may need to cut back on hours. How are you going to make up for the lost revenue? Again, keep working your plan and adjust as necessary. Remember, the goal is zero debt or at least minimal debt.

Here are some additional ideas for students already in college who need more resources.

Military

In chapter four, we discussed military service to pay for your schooling. Some branches of the military have scholarships available for those who are partway through their schooling. Programs vary, and even with a later start into the program, they have the same benefits and drawbacks we discussed earlier.

The one program not already discussed is the US Coast Guard. The Coast Guard offers scholarships for the last two years of college.[53] This money comes with commitments that you must honor, but it's a way to pay for the rest of your college. Besides, the Coast Guard offers a student loan repayment program. I'll cover it in chapter eight.

The Air Force also has a two-year program.[54] The Army has three-year and two-year scholarship programs.[55] The Navy has those same opportunities.[56] And the Marines work through the Navy for their officer training scholarships.[57]

Gap Year or Semester

If you find yourself in a position in which you can either take on student loans or forego the rest of your education, one option is to take some time off. It's important to discuss this idea with your college advisor, as this may have ramifications.

Sometimes family support dries up because of a job loss, financial reversal, or an unwillingness to continue to support your education. Sometimes scholarship rules change. No matter the issue, you need more money to continue your schooling.

Before making this decision, be sure you have ruled out or exhausted all the other options we've discussed. Remember that prayer can help you see where God may make provision. A change in a situation does not surprise Him.

Before you make a gap year decision, consider these disadvantages. When you come back, your school could be more expensive. These days, that's almost a given. But with a decent job, you can quickly overcome the extra expenses, even though your expenses during the following years may continue to rise. Jennifer Williamson listed the possibility that you might never go back to school: "School gets more and more remote as time goes by. For some, one semester can turn into two and more."[58] Taking time off is a risk, particularly if you decide to start a family during your time off from school.

Another risk Ms. Williamson warned of is the possibility of having to start repaying student loans immediately. If you don't have student loans, this is a non-issue. If you've kept your student loan amounts down, this may be an advantage. You could make significant progress by paying down what you have already borrowed, along with saving money for future college costs. Taking time off would be particularly successful if you could save money by living at home during this time.

If you are going to take the break, be sure you can find a good job. Even some college credit on your resume can help you to obtain a better job. And if you look carefully, you may find an employer who helps pay student loans for their employees. See the section on company programs in chapter eight. Or your new employer may help you pay for future schooling. There are many options, but you must look for them.

As in the gap-year discussion in chapter four, use your time off to work and save for future schooling. It's important to resist spending a lot of money on new things for your lifestyle. The goal is a college degree. Keep your goal in sight as you decide to spend versus save. If you're not careful, you could wind up taking out a car loan and putting a lot of items on credit cards. This will get in the way of leaving your job and make it nearly impossible to quit work and go back to school.

One thing your college advisor should discuss with you is the possibility that when you take time off, graduation requirements could change. This would mean you'd need to take more classes. You should also discuss the readmission process. Will you need to start from the beginning, or can you take a formal leave of absence for a specified time?

One nice thing about taking a little time off is that, during time away from the school, you will have a chance to mature and get a better idea of the real world and its foibles. You might even change direction as you interact with people, places, and things.

I took time off from my first college degree. I started part time as a math major (which turned out to be a bad idea) and changed to a music major in my second year. After my first full-time year of college, I took time off to be a musician. What I learned over those years changed my life and started me toward the place I am now. When I went back to school, I was more committed to education and had a better idea of what I wanted to do.

My experience leads to another positive aspect of time off. When you go back to school, you're typically older than many of your peers, which is not a bad thing. Your perspective on college, the work involved, and even the attitudes of those around you will be much different. You'll usually come back with a better work ethic. And being more mature, you'll become an informal leader in many of your classes.

However, your family won't always agree that taking time off from college is a good thing. When I left school to become a musician, I had some unhappy and difficult conversations with my family. For us, it ended well. The days I finally walked across the platforms to get my degrees were happy and proud days for my parents. I was overjoyed to see them so elated.

Work on Campus

Another way to make ends meet during college is to take an on-campus job. Campus food services are usually looking for part-time help, and they are geared to work with students' class and athletic schedules. Having work experience on your resume when you graduate is always helpful, even if it isn't a high-level position. You'll find other jobs on campus too. Several of my students have worked for the school to cover the cost of their classes. Colleges need help in the library, custodial department, and many other areas. For those beyond their freshman year, dorm resident assistant positions usually pay and provide a place to live on campus. Summer jobs are often available on campus and could include housing. You might take a summer class as well, which would apply to your graduation requirements. All these little things can add up to paying for your schooling with no or minimal debt.

EIGHT

Paying Off Your College Debt

I hope the debt load we're addressing here isn't too large. However, the strategies we'll discuss will work for any size debt. The only thing that changes with debt size is the amount of time it will take. First, you need to remember why you should pay off your college debt and why you should do it quickly.

Keep in mind that God owns everything, and He will help us deal with our debt. God is not in the business of deciding people have made a big mess of their lives and making them fix it themselves. No! We serve a generous, forgiving, loving Father who wants to take care of us and rescue us from our troubles. If you don't understand God's love and care, you are burying yourself in a hole from which you will never emerge.

God has promised to care for us. Helping to pay off college loans is part of caring for us. We might not get rid of our debt quickly, and it may take some serious life changes and work on our part. But God will help us just as He helps us in other areas of our lives. He wants us to be free from bondage. College debt (actually, any debt) is bondage. This chapter, along with the resources provided in chapter nine, will outline a number of strategies to eliminate whatever college debt you have generated. The first and foremost strategy is to depend on God while implementing other steps along the way.

Why do we want to be debt free? Because God doesn't want us to be in bondage. He knows that debt of any kind is bondage, and large college debts are debilitating. Large debts of any kind are debilitating. God also wants us to fulfill our promises. When we sign for debt, we agree to pay it off with interest. That's a promise that can be hard to keep. But God not only wants us to keep it, but He also wants to help us keep it.

Teaching

One way to pay off part of your college debt is to teach full-time for five complete and consecutive academic years in a low-income educational or service agency.[59] There is a limit to how much can be repaid, but keep in mind that as you are teaching, you are also earning income. At the same time, you'll have the chance to influence youth who could very well be headed into disastrous lives. This involves more than just paying off college loans. It's an opportunity to influence the next generation positively.

Working in Public Service

Another way to pay off college debt is by working in public service. As of this writing, there are two main ways to do that. The first is to work fulltime for a government agency or certain types of nonprofit organizations.[60] The Federal Student Aid website (see endnote above) indicates what loans are eligible for forgiveness and explains how to apply. The drawback is that you need to work for the government agency or nonprofit organization for ten years before the repayment program will begin. During those ten years, you must keep up with regular payments on your loans.

Public service loan forgiveness sounds like a restrictive program. But since the government provided over 22 million jobs in 2016,[61] and the nonprofit sector provided over 12.3 million jobs[62] in 2017, there are lots of opportunities in many different job types and specialties. The key is perseverance. Also, keep in mind the typical job security of government work.

Perkins Loan Cancellation

If you have a Perkins Loan, you might meet their terms for forgiveness of the loan while working in some specific vocations.[63] The vocations include jobs at a child or family services agency, firefighter, faculty member at a tribal college, certain jobs at a Title I school, teacher, or public defender. This is not a complete list, but it gives you an idea of the kinds of vocations that qualify.

Nurses' Debt Forgiveness

"Thanks to state-specific and federal initiatives, nurses have access to some of the best student loan forgiveness programs out there."[64] Nurses have access to the public service loan forgiveness program as well as specialized programs, including the Nurse Corps Loan Repayment Program, the National Health Service Corps Loan Repayment Program, and the Perkins Loan Cancellation for Nurses. Each has restrictions and rules, but they are out there and are legitimate ways to repay student loans.

Student Disability

If you have federal student loans and have become permanently and totally disabled, there is a debt relief program for you. The rules and processes are complicated and the burden of proof high. Disability forgiveness is not something you want to use, but if it's needed, it's there.[65]

Death of the Student

There is a forgiveness program for outstanding debt if a student or his or her parents have taken out federal loans to pay for the student's education and the student dies. Without this program, federal student loans could be a claim on the student's estate, and parents might still need to repay loans they incurred for their child. Like forgiveness of a loan for disability, this is a program no one wants to have to use.

Filing Bankruptcy

Keep in mind what I said at the beginning of this chapter about God's principles and keeping your promises. When you took out your student loans, you promised to repay them. Bankruptcy may sound like a good option, but it may not be an option at all.

Typically, federal student loans cannot be discharged in bankruptcy. However, if you can prove undue hardship in bankruptcy court, it is rare but possible to have a full discharge of your federal student loans.[66]

If you or your parents took out loans from a bank or other lending institution outside of the federal government, those could typically be discharged through bankruptcy. One thing to keep in mind is that because something may be legal doesn't automatically make it right. When we look at what God's Word says about it, we see that bankruptcy is a decision that needs to be approached with caution, good biblical counsel, and much prayer.

Forgiveness at the End
of an Income-driven Payment Plan

"If your federal student loan payments are high compared to your income, you may want to repay your loans under an income-driven repayment plan."[67] One of the options upon graduation is to enroll in an income-driven repayment plan. This allows student loan payments based upon your income. As with all federal programs, it has rules and limitations. The big benefit of this program is that, when you have made all your payments according to the program's rules and the term of the program has come, whatever principal balance is left on your loan is forgiven. However, the complete term of the loan will most likely be over twenty years.

State-Specific Programs

Several individual states have student loan forgiveness programs for a surprising variety of reasons. For example, California and Ohio offer loan forgiveness for medical graduates. New York offers loan forgiveness for farmers, and Pennsylvania offers forgiveness for lawyers.[68] There may be others, and like other forgiveness programs, they have specific rules and constraints.

Surviving the Closing of Your College While You Were Attending

Thankfully, it's rare to hear of a college closing while students still attend. But a few highly publicized college closures in the last decade have left many students with a partial education and the student debt incurred to pay for it. Should that happen, check into a program that forgives federal loans taken out to pay for the schooling. To use this program, contact the company that services your loan. If you have private loans, you will probably have to pay them off in full.

Military Service

College graduates can take advantage of a specific US Coast Guard program in which the Coast Guard makes their college loan payments.[69] This program includes people working on bachelor's degrees or master's degrees. The graduate must make a commitment to the Coast Guard, and there are both benefits and draw-backs. These are listed in chapter four under the topic of "Military." The program includes an officer's commission in the Coast Guard. It also requires an excellent student record, as shown by grades and leadership distinction.

The Army, Navy, and Air Force have loan repayment programs. The terms vary, and there are restrictions on which loans are eligible for repayment. As with other military programs, the graduate must make a commitment to the branch of service chosen. Military recruitment centers will provide details.

Company Programs

In the competitive environment for good employees, some companies now offer to make payments on their employees' student loans. The December 26, 2017, issue of *Forbes* magazine carried an article on what they called the "Just 100." The topic of college debt repayment was part of that article. Regrettably, it's beyond the scope of this book to provide a list of these companies, due partly to the fact that the list may change significantly in a short period of time. But don't hesitate to find out if your employer or potential employer would help you with your loans.

Ministries

Since college debt has made missionary or overseas relief worker recruitment difficult, some ministries help college graduates become free to follow where God would call them. Leigh Jones wrote an article for *World Magazine*, referencing a ministry raising money to pay off college debt for those going into Christian overseas work.[70] The ministry in the article may not be the only one doing that, but if your goal is missions or overseas relief work, some detailed research may be in order.

Taking Steps to Eliminate Debt
by Making Payments

While it's true that God wants to provide for us to get out of debt, making payments is probably the most common path to eliminating the debt. Biblical stewardship is the key. You have debt. God loves you and wants to provide for you to get out of debt. You now need to follow His principles as He provides for you to get out of the debt you have taken on.

The first step in this process is to recognize God's ownership of everything, including our stuff, our skills, our natural abilities, our education, our relationships, and our future. Once we grasp God's ownership, our circumstances begin to look a lot less depressing. And we all know a crushing load of debt is tremendously depressing. We take this step by emotionally transferring ownership of everything we have, including our possessions, our talents, our education, and our future to God. We don't make out new deeds to our house or change the title on our cars, but in our hearts, we acknowledge God's ownership of everything. He certainly owns enough to help us as we take steps to pay off our debt.

The next step is to pray. Actually, we should pray continually, not only through paying off college debt but through our entire lives. If God owns everything, we should seek His direction about managing all those things. We are biblical stewards and need to act that way.

> ### Three Practical Steps
> ### To Get Out of Debt
> 1. Stop overspending
> 2. Start repaying
> 3. Don't borrow more

The *How to Manage Your Money Workbook*[71] lists three steps to get out of debt. It sounds simple, and it is: "Stop overspending, start repaying what you owe, and don't borrow any more." The workbook also pointed out that, if it took more than a month to get into debt, it will probably take more than a month to get back out.

Before getting into practical suggestions to make this process more successful, I'll cover some additional principles that will help to make this process possible. These are all listed in the *How to Manage Your Money Workbook*.[72] They are all part of becoming a biblical steward, which will revolutionize your life. If you are married, it will revolutionize your marriage. It did for my life and my marriage.

The first principle is to accept God's provision. This means we don't constantly look longingly beyond our financial situation. Accepting God's provision is counterintuitive to the world, which strives to make more money and sometimes gets into serious trouble in the process. God gives us peace when we stay within His plan and make the best of what He provides. I discussed deferred gratification in the chapter four section on spousal support. It's also part of the concept of accepting what God has provided.

The next principal is also a practical step: refuse to make quick decisions. All too often, quick decisions result in impulse purchases. In chapter nine, I'll discuss ways to protect ourselves from impulse purchases and quick decisions.

Next, excel in your work. From a practical standpoint, doing well at your work should result in pay increases or promotions or bonuses. None of those are guaranteed, but every time you get a pay increase, promotion, or bonus, you're a step closer to paying off your debt.

Then make sure to have a clean conscience. Confess your sins and make restitution to those you have harmed. Prayer is a critical step in this process. Psalm 66:18 tells us if we cherished sin in our heart, the Lord would not have listened to our prayers. If we have wronged someone by overt action or even accidentally, we need to make it right. After we make it right as best as we can, God will hear our prayers.

The next principal, contentment, is not something we hear much about these days. Our culture doesn't promote it and, regrettably, we don't often discuss it at church. But Paul wrote to the Philippians, "For I have learned to be content whatever the circumstances. I know what it is to be in need, and I know what it is to have plenty. I have learned the secret of being content in any and every situation, whether well fed or hungry, whether living in plenty or in want" (Philippians 4:11–12). Until we learn to be content with God's provision, we could be tempted to misuse money He provided to help pay off college debt, derailing the debt payment plan. In chapter nine, we'll also discuss making a debt-payment plan.

The principle of balance in our commitments is our next action. At this point, you may ask what balance has to do with paying off debt. Remember, we are talking about biblical stewardship. And a large portion of biblical stewardship is keeping our lives in line with what God has for us. God wants us to lead balanced lives and avoid the frustration and problems that come from having too many balls in the air.

I learned to juggle "balls" (commitments and tasks) early in life. But when I overdid it and dropped one of the balls, it usually fell on my foot and hurt. Keep Proverbs 23:4–5 in mind: "Do not wear yourself out to get rich; do not trust your own cleverness. Cast but a glance at riches, and they are gone, for they will surely sprout wings and fly off to the sky like an eagle."

Many readers will probably consider this next principal as meddling. All I can say to that is, "Oh, well." This last principle is the sacrifice of desires. Please don't get this wrong. If God puts a desire in your heart, no matter what it might be, you should not sacrifice it. However, if you have taken on debt, you may need to postpone the fulfillment of a godly desire. God is capable of ensuring you are where He wants you to be, when He wants you to be there. Don't try to make it happen yourself.

The desires we typically need to sacrifice are the extravagances and foolish sensualism promoted in our culture. We must eliminate the "I deserve it!" mentality from our lives. Things do not fulfill us. Only a relationship with God will fulfill us. And He loves to fulfill us. As we finish this last principal, a comment from Solomon, the wisest man who ever lived, might help bring things into perspective.

I denied myself nothing my eyes desired; I refused my heart no pleasure. My heart took delight in all my labor, and this was the reward for all my toil. Yet when I surveyed all that my hands had done and what I had toiled to achieve, everything was meaningless, a chasing after the wind; nothing was gained under the sun. (Ecclesiastes 2:10–11)

I should warn you that implementing these principles will probably take the rest of your life. The point is to get started, to make changes in your habits, and let God take care of changing your life. It's a trite saying, but true—every journey begins with the first step.

With these principles in mind, we can take practical steps to eliminate our college debt. Remember that prayer is an important part of the process. So don't stop praying.

The first practical step is to establish written plans and goals. Writing things down or typing them onto my computer or cell phone is an essential part of achieving my objectives. My wife and I have spent much time and prayer in deciding the direction for our lives. To a large extent, we were poster children for the proverb, "In their hearts humans plan their course, but the Lord establishes their steps" (Proverbs 16:9). We made our plans, we wrote them down, we started to follow those plans, and the Lord often took us in a different direction. While it was sometimes frustrating, the Lord knew what He was doing, and we are glad for the redirects.

A part of those plans is to learn to trust God. I don't know of a better way to learn to trust God than to give Him the first portion of everything He provides. His provision includes our salary, money from extra work, earnings on investments, and sometimes even gifts from other people. Keep this in mind: God's provision most often comes through God's people. Proverbs 3:9–10 says, "Honor the Lord with your wealth, with the firstfruits of all your crops; then your barns will be filled to overflowing, and your vats will brim over with new wine." For us, giving the first portion is typically our giving at our church. Giving the first portion of your income is often referred to as a tithe.

Tithing is a subject of much controversy in the church. Since I don't want to get into the tithe debate here, let's just look at the bottom line of giving. In giving the first portion of God's provision, we literally show God how much we trust Him to provide, and that even without the first portion, we will have enough. It's a step of faith, and frankly, it's a no-lose situation. In Malachi 3:10, God said, "'Bring the whole tithe into the storehouse, that there may be food in my house. Test me in this,' says the Lord Almighty, 'and see if I will not throw open the floodgates of heaven and pour out so much blessing that there will not be room enough to store it.'" God tells us we can test Him on this. And if we do, He will pour out blessings on us. Please don't

---

Plans to Eliminate Debt

- Establish written plans and goals
- Trust God through giving
- Control or eliminate the use of credit
- Learn to be content
- Seek godly counselt

get me wrong. This promise is not a "give to get" message. It is a message of provision, and when you are in debt, you certainly need God's provision.

The next practical suggestion is to control or eliminate the use of credit. Credit here includes credit cards, home equity lines of credit, personal loans, car loans, and mortgages. In chapter nine, you will find a resource illustration on how to buy a home with minimal debt. And because you may have a large chunk of college debt, it could be quite a while until you're in a position to own a home. Most people don't want to hear this, but when signing onto a student loan, you're making decisions for the future. This could include putting off buying a home, putting off marriage, and putting off other dreams or life directions.

With a new college degree and a decent job, you will probably receive all kinds of offers from people who want to loan you money, from basic credit cards to personal lines of credit. The best thing to do with them is to shred them. The shredding of credit card offers is also one of the many steps involved in combating identity theft.

You will probably also be told you must take out debt to get a credit score. Noted financial author Dave Ramsey calls the credit score, "an I-love-debt score."[73] He went on to say, "The only way to have a good credit score is to go into debt, stay in debt, and continually pay your accounts perfectly—without adding too much debt or paying too much off." Isn't the point of this book to get out of debt?

It is possible to operate without a credit card. A debit card is a great substitute and won't allow you to spend more than you have in the bank. By avoiding the temptation to overspend, you will help yourself to follow the principle of being content. If you feel you need a credit card for transactions like renting a car or traveling, you will need to discipline yourself to pay off the balance every month. Never carry a balance and never pay interest. And when you are not traveling or renting a car, keep the credit card in your safe deposit box. Keep the temptation out of easy reach.

The next practical suggestion is to learn to be content. If you have more student loans than you can comfortably pay after you've met your other obligations, the solution is not a better job or more income. The best solution is to figure out a way to be content with what you have and to live on less than you make. In chapter nine, you'll learn how striving for additional income to make ends meet impacts a family.

To reach contentment, the first step is to reduce expenses. Author Charles Dickens (1812–1870) wrote the following line for one of his characters: "Annual income twenty pounds, annual expenditure nineteen six, result happiness. Annual income twenty pounds, annual expenditure twenty pounds ought and six, result misery" (*David Copperfield*, 1849). In today's vernacular, it's more like "Annual income $20,000, annual expenditure $19,600, result happiness. Annual income $20,000, annual expenditure $20,600, result misery." Spending more than you earn is a path to disaster and unhappiness.

The next step in learning contentment is to pray and give God an opportunity to provide what you need. We have a loving heavenly Father who delights in providing for us. And He can provide in many ways. We always need to trust and often need to wait. If you had waited and not just taken the loans for your college debt, would you be in the situation you're now in?

Part of contentment and part of having plans is to be sure your plans are from God, not from your neighbor, the commercial, the pressure at work to conform, or any other worldly source. Jeremiah wrote, "'For I know the plans I have for you,' declares the Lord, 'plans to prosper you and not to harm you, plans to give you hope and a future'" (Jeremiah 29:11). I don't think we can say it too many times: God loves us and wants to care for us. God's care includes provision.

In the process of determining God's goals for you, one step (after prayer) is to seek godly counsel. Proverbs 15:22 says, "Plans fail for lack of counsel, but with many advisers they succeed." If nothing else, this verse tells us we should seek counsel. We cannot possibly know the right answers to all the questions, or even all the potential answers to all the questions. In the writing of this book, I sought counsel from trusted friends. You can find scriptures relating to counsel in the Scripture Appendix.

Of course, our best counselor is God. Proverbs 8:14 says, "Counsel and sound judgment are mine; I have insight." The lesson is always to check the counsel you receive against what God says in His Word, the Bible.

The bottom line: trust God for His provision to help you pay off your debt. He can do it, and you need to be wise in handling His provision. The principles and strategies laid out in this chapter will help you get there. In the following chapter, you'll find more specific tools you can use to get to debt-free status.

When you achieve freedom from debt and trust God for His provision, your life will change. The freedom you gain, after being set free from the bondage to debt, is almost unbelievable. Once you have gotten there, don't go back into debt for anything. Follow the advice in the book of Galatians, "It is for freedom that Christ has set us free. Stand firm, then, and do not let yourselves be burdened again by a yoke of slavery" (Galatians 5:1).

Consequences of Not Paying Off Your College Debt

As with most debts, there are consequences for failing to make payments. In the case of federal student loans, the government has special tools available to help them collect what is owed. Although there are ways that student loans can be forgiven, the path toward that forgiveness can be very narrow and restrictive. If you don't meet all the conditions, the debt is not likely to be forgiven. Federal student loans are typically not dissolved in bankruptcy, either. The rules there are technical, and you should seek legal advice if you think you're going to go in the direction of bankruptcy.

A creditor can pursue several different avenues of collection. Usually, collections start with phone calls or letters requesting or demanding payment. Receiving a letter from a creditor requesting or demanding payment can be a very distressing situation. We all like to think of ourselves as dependable, as persons of our word, of integrity. Receiving a creditor phone call or letter can shake those beliefs. Should the letter from the creditor be ineffective, many creditors will turn the debt over to a debt-collection agency. The creditor will probably get less of the money due to them but will be happy to get something.

Garnishments

Webster's defines a garnishment as "a stoppage of a specified sum from wages to satisfy a creditor or a legal obligation (such as child support)". Garnishments are allowed to be up to 50% of your wages. The garnishment is most often accomplished by taking the amount determined by the court directly out of your paycheck before you get your pay. You just get your net pay, less whatever the garnishment is.

Debt collectors are required to follow certain rules. However, some debt collectors have been known to violate those rules, making the creditor's life miserable. Someone in this position may want to seek legal help in dealing with unscrupulous debt collectors.

Usually, the final step in a debt-collection procedure is a lawsuit. Since the student or the student's parents agreed to make payments on those loans, the lawsuit will probably be successful, and the company or debt collector will gain access to assets owned by the student or the parents or to future income earned by the student or the parents. If you lose the lawsuit, the court can order garnishment, which means a payment is taken out of your regular paycheck before the paycheck even gets to you. The court determines the amount of the garnishment.

One more thing to know about falling behind on debt payments is that being delinquent on your payments can affect your life in many ways. If you don't make payments as agreed, this usually shows up on your credit report. Landlords now check credit reports before renting an apartment, car dealers check before selling a car, and insurance agents check before issuing a policy. Even employers check credit records before offering a job. If someone will loan money to a student or parents who have defaulted on a loan, the interest rate for the new loan will typically be much higher than they'd be for someone who has made all payments on time and as agreed upon.

If the loan in default is a federal student loan, the government has the option of holding back income tax refunds to help pay the balance due on the loan. They can also hold back other federal payments such as Social Security retirement or disability payments and can declare the student ineligible for any future student loans.[74] The government also has the same legal options in debt collection as any other creditor.

NINE

Practical Resources

Prayer

Once again, the first practical resource you have is prayer. While it may seem redundant to say this again, it's important enough to reemphasize. God is capable of helping you to eliminate your college debt in ways you can't even imagine. So keep praying while you implement the practical steps below.

In the prior chapter, we recognized that God does not hear our prayers if we harbor sin in our hearts. The principles in this book will work for anyone, but if you want to make the best use of those principles, you need to know their Author, the Creator of the world. The incredible thing is that God wants you to know Him personally, not just know about Him.

From the beginning of time, God knew you would read this book. If you don't know Him, He knew this section would be here, inviting you to know Him. Knowing God is not a set of rules or list of things you shouldn't do. Knowing God is first knowing that His Son, Jesus Christ, died for your sins and imperfections. He told us in the Bible that "all have sinned and fall short of the glory of God" (Romans 3:23). Next, ask for His forgiveness for those sins and imperfections, and accept His forgiveness. First John 1:9 tells us, "If we confess our sins, He is faithful and just and will forgive us our sins and purify us from all unrighteousness." Not only did Christ die to take away the guilt and penalty of your sins, but He rose from the grave so you might have new life, so God would look on you as perfect, and so you might no longer fear death or any other power in this life. This new life reaches down into the corners and hidden places of who we are and transforms even how we think about the change in our pockets.

I took the step of accepting Christ's forgiveness at the beginning of my senior year of high school. I had lived a good life and had been taught that I was okay with God because I was a good person. Then I learned about Ephesians 2:8–9 (ESV): "For by grace you have been saved through faith. And this is not your own doing; it is the gift of God, not a result of works, so that no one may boast." I realized all my good works were of no account. I needed to do as Romans 10:9 (ESV) said: "Confess with your mouth that Jesus is Lord and believe in your heart that God raised him from the dead, you will be saved." I did believe and confess and am now so thankful that "God so loved the world, that he gave his only Son, that whoever believes in him should not perish but have eternal life" (John 3:16 ESV). I committed my life to God about fifty years ago and have never regretted it.

It's that simple and it's that beautiful. God doesn't want to make knowing Him hard or confusing. However, if you take these steps, it's important to become a part of a community that places a high value applying God's Word (the Bible) to our lives. Being involved in a Christian community will enable you to learn more about God and to know Him better. A relationship with Christ extends far beyond merely paying off college loans.

Setting Goals

You probably can't achieve many of your goals until you are financially free. Author, radio personality, co-founder of Crown Financial Ministries, and my mentor, Larry Burkett, used to say no one can be spiritually free until they are financially free. Financial freedom doesn't necessarily mean debt free, but it does mean your financial life is under control. The bottom line is living within your means. Co-founder of Crown Financial Ministries, radio personality, and author Howard Dayton suggested that you "act your own wage."[75]

To live within our means, we must make an important decision. It would be easier if we had to make it only once, but we must deal with it continually. The issue is defining our needs versus our wants. One wise teacher defined needs as "the purchases necessary to provide your basic requirements such as food, clothing, home, medical coverage, and others."[76] Things beyond this are often called wants or desires. We can call those desires by many different names, but if you live on a tight spending plan with significant debt, you must avoid or defer those desires. When you accepted college debt, you made a decision that going to college was more important than spending money on desires when payments were due on the loan. As a result, until the loan is paid, only the needs can be part of your spending plan.

Creating a Plan for Spending and Debt Elimination

When you create a budget (or spending plan, as I prefer to call it), you have only four spending divisions at the start. In the future, you may have a fifth. The four divisions (in order of importance) are giving, taxes, family needs, and debts. Please notice the word next to family is needs, not wants or desires. While you are in debt, particularly heavily in debt, you must prioritize debt elimination over wants or desires. As you faithfully follow your spending plan, you will eventually have a surplus. Then you will be at the fifth division of income: your surplus.

If you just graduated from college and are entering your post-college life, you have a wonderful opportunity to start off right. Now that you have a job, you know how much income you have, or at least you have a good idea. Incomes can fluctuate depending on your job and whether you are eligible for overtime or other factors.

If you have been out of college for a while, have a job, and want to gain control of your life, you will have an even better idea of the income available to parcel out to those four divisions.

Step One: List Your Debts

It's critical to understand your starting point. If you have taken on college debt (or any debt), write it down on paper or enter it into a computer document. If you have credit card balances, include them. If you have personal loans from family or friends, include them too. And if you have a car loan, put that down. On this page, you'll find an easy-to-use form titled "List of Debts." The source for most of these forms is the *Family Financial Workbook*.[77] The workbook also includes instructions for completing each form. This form is also available in the Forms and Tools Appendix. You can also access it at www.SayNoTo CollegeDebt.com. Here you'll find a number of Excel workbook budget forms, including this one.

LIST OF DEBTS as of _____					
Creditor/ Purchase	Monthly payment	Balance due	Payment date	Payoff date	Interest rate

Instructions are included with the forms, both in the appendix and on the website. In addition, the website has a link to video instructions on completing each form.

If you're married, an important principle comes into play as you fill in this form. In the book of Genesis, God revealed part of His plan for marriage: "A man leaves his father and mother and is united to his wife, and they become one flesh" (Genesis 2:24). Becoming one flesh is more than just a physical act. Becoming one flesh also includes unifying your finances. This can be difficult if someone has been financially hurt in a prior relationship or was brought up in a home in which a parent used money as a weapon.

Many financial experts discourage lumping all the income, money, and debts together. But based on what I see in God's design, all aspects of a couple's lives need to be brought together to have a complete marriage. One financial counselor said having separate banking accounts "makes about as much sense as maintaining separate houses."[78] A his-money-her-money philosophy often leads to a him-versus-her mentality. Keeping finances separate does not lead to a lasting marriage. If you feel like merging your finances is not possible in your marriage, it might be time to talk to a pastor or biblical marriage counselor. After you have created your list of debts, you can start creating a spending plan.

Step Two: Create a Spending Plan

To create a spending plan, sit down with a copy of the Monthly Estimated Budget form or an Excel workbook in front of you. The source for most of these forms is the *Family Financial Workbook.*[79] The workbook is an excellent resource and goes into these steps in more depth. If you are married, both you and your spouse must participate. This form is available in the Forms and Tools Appendix and at www.SayNoToCollegeDebt.com.

MONTHLY ESTIMATED BUDGET
AS OF _____

Monthly Income
GROSS INCOME PER MONTH:
Salary
Interest
Dividends
Other
Total Gross Income Per Month

LESS:
1. **Tithe/Giving**

2. **Tax (Fed, State, FICA)**

Net Spendable Income

Monthly Living Expenses
3. **Housing**
Mortgage
Insurance
Taxes
Electricity
Gas
Water
Sanitation
Telephone
Maintenance
Assoc, Dues
Other
Total Housing

4. **Food**

5. **Automobile**
Payments
Gas & Oil
Insurance
License/Taxes
Maint/Repair
Replace
Total Automobile

6. **Insurance**
Life
Medical
Other
Total Insurance

7. **Debts**
Credit Cards
Loans & Notes
Other
Total Debts

8. **Entertainment & Recreation**
Eating Out
Baby Sitters
Activities/Trips
Vacation
Other
Total Entertain & Recreation

9. **Clothing**

10. **Savings**

11. **Medical Expenses**
Doctor
Dentist
Prescriptions
Other
Total Medical Expenses

12. **Miscellaneous**
Cosmetics
Beauty, Barber
Laundry, Clean
Allowances
Pets
Subscriptions
Gifts
Christmas Gifts
Other
Total Miscellaneous

13. **Investments**

14. **School / Child Care**
Tuition
Materials
Transportation
Day Care
Total School / Child Care

TOTAL LIVING EXPENSES

Income Versus Living Expenses

Net Spendable Income
Less

Total Living Expenses

Surplus or Deficit

Since I've been speaking of marriage, I should add that piling wedding debt on top of college debt can do serious damage to a new marriage. Weddings do not have to be expensive. Many brides dream of a fairytale wedding, but fairytale weddings usually cost a lot. When couples go into significant debt to fund this fairytale wedding, the wonderful dream can quickly turn into a nightmare. This is another areas in which we must seriously examine our needs and wants.

Step Three: Bringing the Spending Plan into Balance

Let me make a wild guess. Once you've completed the Monthly Estimated Budget form, you'll see that you have more money going out every month than coming in, and the number on the bottom line is negative. Regrettably, this is not an uncommon problem.

In dealing with this, you have several options. First, and most important, don't give up hope. Remember, you're depending on God. So keep praying. You can take other steps too. First, tweak your spending plan by cutting unnecessary expenditures. The Budget Analysis form will help you. As with the other forms, it's from the *Family Financial Workbook,*[80] in the appendix, and at www.SayNoToCollegeDebt.com.

The instructions will help you modify your spending plan to try to bring it into balance. As a new graduate, even with a college degree, you'll need to work hard to reduce spending. At this point, you'll have a degree but not a lot of experience, so you must live on an entry-level salary.

Go through the process and see how close you can come to reasonably balancing your spending plan. If you succeed, you can move to the next step. In case you can't bring your spending plan into balance, I've included a couple more ideas that might help.

First, if you followed the recommended order for taking out student loans (chapter three), you started with federal loans. If you have federal loans, you might be able to reduce or defer payments because of hardship. Check with the person who services your loan and find out how to defer or reduce payments temporarily and bring your spending plan into balance. Keep the words "temporarily reduce your payment" in mind as you progress on your debt paydown effort. Later in this section, I will provide a caution about doing this.

If you have a car loan and it contributes to the negative number at the bottom of your spending plan, you can contact your bank about adjusting your payments. Some banks can and will adjust payments. Again, see my caution about reducing payments. If the bank won't or can't work adjust the payments, you might need to sell the car and replace it with an older, dependable vehicle.

Working with credit card companies is a little tougher. You can contact the credit card issuers and ask for temporarily deferred or reduced payments. Resist the urge to refinance your debt. The drawback to refinancing, deferring, or reducing payments is that interest accumulates all the while you are making payments. If you stretch out your payments, you add to the total amount your debts will ultimately cost you. Remember this caution when deferring school loans, modifying car payments, or negotiating credit card payments.

As a last resort, think about increasing your income. Later in this chapter, you'll find a section that shows the pros and cons of using additional income to balance your spending plan. Please be sure and look at the extra income section below before you apply for an additional job.

After trying the above suggestions, redo your Budget Analysis form to show your spending plan in balance. Then redo your Monthly Estimated Budget form with your new numbers. In the next section, we will look at how to administer your new spending plan.

Step Four: Tracking Your Spending

A spending plan is a huge waste of time and creates frustration if you never take it out of the desk drawer. There are many ways to keep track of spending, from a manual system to a mostly automated system. No matter what system you choose, you need to take time to manage it. Some people think administering a

Monthly Budget Worksheet
Month of _____

Category>	Income	1. Tithe/Giv.	2. Taxes	3. Housing	4. Food	5. Auto	6. Insur	7. Debt	8. Ent/Rec	9. Clothing	10. Savings	11. Medical	12. Misc	13. Invest	14. Sch/Chld
Budgeted Amount>	$	$	$	$	$	$	$	$	$	$	$	$	$	$	$
Day of Month															
1															
2															
3															
4															
5															
6															
7															
8															
9															
10															
11															
12															
13															
14															
15															
MTD Subtotal															
16															
17															
18															
19															
20															
21															
22															
23															
24															
25															
26															
27															
28															
29															
30															
31															
Month Total															
Surplus/Def															
YTD Budget															
YTD Total Actl															
YTD Surpl/Def															

Budget Summary

This Month
Total Income $ _____
Minus Total Spending $ _____
Equals Surplus/Deficit $ _____

+

Prior Year-To-Date
Total Income $ _____
Minus Total Spending $ _____
Equals Surplus/Deficit $ _____

=

Year-To-Date
Total Income $ _____
Minus Total Spending $ _____
Equals Surplus/Deficit $ _____

spending plan is wasted time. But if you want to get out of the bondage of debt, you'll need discipline, and the time spent is part of the discipline. This step is important, so don't overlook it or put it aside. You can find good online programs to help you maintain your spending plan. Some are free, and some require monthly payments. It's beyond the scope of this book to recommend specific products. The reviews of the program will help you choose. If you don't want to use online tools, you can use computer workbooks or paper forms. The Monthly Budget Workbook form pictured on the previous page is available in the Forms and Tools Appendix and at www.SayNoToCollegeDebt.com. It is from *Do Well—the Crown Biblical Financial Study.*[81]

Use this form every month to list your income and expenditures by day and by category. When you total it at the bottom, you'll know how you've done that month. The boxes at the bottom summarize and keep track of the year-to-date comparison of income to expenses. Be sure to follow the step-by-step instructions in the Forms and Tools Appendix or at www.SayNoToCollege Debt.com.

Managing the Spending Plan and Debt Elimination Process

Before I list a few ways to make your debt paydown more successful, you need to know this system will require adjustments as you go along. When you start, create your Monthly Estimated Budget as if you'll use it the entire year. Realistically, you can expect to get two or three months out of your first pass at a Monthly Estimated Budget. By then, you'll have discovered more information, and you can see how your spending plan is working. With that new knowledge, go back and redo the step to create a new spending plan. With the revised data in the revised spending plan, you can use it at least six more months. Then do the process again and use that plan for another year. As you get better at the process, you'll get better results. You should soon be able to create a spending plan that will be good for an entire year.

As you create and work the spending plan as outlined above, be sure you emphasize paying down debt. Along the way, you'll be tempted to let debt payments slide. This is when you need what financial author and radio personality Dave Ramsey calls "gazelle intensity."[82]

Gazelle intensity is a mindset that helps you realize getting out of debt is a lifesaver. The gazelle is the potential prey of the cheetah, the fastest animal on earth. The gazelle watches closely to spot the cheetah before it gets close enough to catch it. In ridding ourselves of the bondage of debt, we need the same intensity toward anything that would sneak up on us and derail our plan. Ramsey said, "The level of gazelle intensity varies from person to person and situation to situation. But the more intense you get about paying off your debt, the quicker you'll be free from it! Think about everything else you could do with money currently owed—like saving, investing, and building for your children's future."[83]

In the next section, we'll look at more specialized tools to help you stay on course to reach the goal of being debt-free. Now that you have a spending plan and goals in place, you are already well along the road to financial freedom. And financial freedom is a big part of spiritual freedom.

Using Tools for Specific Parts of Your Debt-elimination Process

At www.SayNoToCollegeDebt.com, you'll find links to many videos that will help you understand the tools covered below. I also have links to many other videos, covering other aspects of God's principles for handling money. Please feel free to watch them as many times as you want. Tell your friends. I don't know anyone who wouldn't benefit from hearing God's principles for his or her life.

Extra Income

Taking a second job as a way to earn extra income has both pros and cons. This should not be your first choice because it causes a couple of big problems. First, extra income is always taxed at your highest incremental tax rate. Since tax rates change, the best I can use here are tax rates current at this writing.

Say a single person in California, who already earns $35,000 increases her income by $10,000 with a second job. This will net only a little over $7,000. Her additional estimated federal taxes on the extra $10,000 will be about $1,750. Additional state taxes on the $10,000 will be about $350, additional FICA taxes: $620, additional Medicare taxes: $145, and additional state disability taxes: $90. These taxes greatly shrink the take-home pay. If you thought you would earn $20 per hour, look again. The net is only about $14 per hour.

Additionally, other costs crop up with a second job. These include things like extra gas in your car, possibly new clothing, and extra meals out because you get home tired from your second job. Pile onto those costs the little things typically going on at work, like coworkers' birthday gifts, collections for an employee who's retiring, and participation in other workplace activities. It all adds up.

If you are married, extra income almost always takes a toll on the family. Most second jobs are on nights and weekends, the only times most families have together. Is the extra money worth the price your family pays? Psalm 127:1–2 (NASB) says, "Unless the Lord builds the house, They labor in vain who build it; Unless the

Lord guards the city, The watchman keeps awake in vain. It is vain for you to rise up early, To retire late, To eat the bread of painful labors; For He gives to His beloved even in his sleep."

If you can earn extra income through an increase in salary or by getting a better-paying job, it might work. You still lose the tax part, but the cost to your family is not increased.

One situation in which you might want to consider a temporary extra job is when you have a payment coming up that's going to be hard to make, or when you can't make progress paying down one nagging bill. To deal with this kind of short-term issue, a temporary job might help. The downsides listed above will still be there, but if you were to deliver pizza, teach English as a second language, or apply for holiday employment, the impact on your family should be short and minimal.

Once you have taken care of your nagging bill or payment, you can go back to a more normal routine, which includes time with your family and friends. Most family and friends will understand your absence to deal with a crisis, and you can reintegrate quickly. Be careful not to get used to the extra money and decide to keep the job. The impacts on relationships could be bigger than you can imagine.

Debt Paydown

This section will walk you through an efficient plan to pay down debt. This plan assumes you have more than just student debt, but you can use some of these suggestions even if you have only student debt.

Assume John Smith has several debts, listed below. Since he lives with gazelle intensity, we can be sure this list is complete. We've listed the debts from highest balance to lowest balance. If John had a mortgage, it would probably be at the top of the list. But since he is a new graduate, he doesn't have a mortgage.

LIST OF DEBTS —John Smith as of December 1, 20XX (year he graduated)					
Creditor/ Purchase	Monthly payment	Balance due	Payment date	Payoff date	Interest rate
Nat'l School Loan	$1,007.94	$95,030.00	3rd	11/3/XX	5%
Simple Auto Fin.	321.00	11,688.85	15th	8/15/XX	11.5%
QBank	129.14	4,304.80	17th	7/17/XX	24%
Nordstrom's	18.90	902.58	25th	2/25/XX	21%
Dr. Tabb (dentist)	20.00	60.00	1st	2/1/XX	0%
TOTALS	$1,496.98	$111,986.23			

It's important to total the monthly payments and balance-due columns. To get started, he commits to himself (and maybe an accountability partner) that he will never pay less than $1,496.98 until these debts are paid. He also commits to not adding any new spending or increases in his lifestyle until these debts are paid. If he has a net increase in salary, he will use the increase to pay these debts.

This method is contrary to the world's ways, but we aren't to be of the world. We live here for a season and should follow God's principles. It works like this. For the next three months, John makes all the monthly payments, as shown on the List of Debts. After three months of paying $20 per month to his dentist, this debt is paid. Since John has committed never to pay less than the $1,496.98, he adds this $20 per month to his minimum payment to Nordstrom's. He also uses his biggest, blackest marker to cross the dentist off his list. He could redo the List of Debts, but that would create unnecessary work. Instead, he should cross out $18.90 in the Nordstrom's box and write in $38.90 instead. See the altered form on the next page:

LIST OF DEBTS —John Smith as of December 1, 20XX (year he graduated)					
Creditor/ Purchase	Monthly payment	Balance due	Payment date	Payoff date	Interest rate
Nat'l School Loan	$1,007.94	$95,030.00	3rd	11/3/XX	5%
Simple Auto Fin.	321.00	11,688.85	15th	8/15/XX	11.5%
QBank	129.14	4,304.80	17th	7/17/XX	24%
Nordstrom's	38.90 ~~18.90~~	902.58	25th	2/25/XX	21%
Dr. Tabb (dentist)	~~20.00~~	~~60.00~~	~~1st~~	~~2/1/XX~~	~~0%~~
TOTALS	$1,496.98	$111,986.23			

Notice, he still pays $1,496.98 per month. He has more than doubled the payment on the Nordstrom's card, since he no longer has to pay Dr. Tabb. Also, the Nordstrom's balance dropped a little from the regular payments John made while paying off Dr. Tabb. That should save him more than half of the payments he still needs to make on the Nordstrom's card.

Now let's say God decides to intervene in the process some months down the road and prompts John's maiden aunt to give him $1,000 to help him get his life started. After John gives the first part of God's provision to his church, he has $900 left to spend. The issue of giving is covered in the *Family Financial Workbook* and other writings by many other good authors. It's one of God's principles, and I covered it in chapter nine.

Again, if John were a typical person in the world, he would take a vacation or buy a big-screen TV or some other indulgence. But John runs with gazelle intensity and has determined that getting out of debt is much more important than having more toys. He takes the $900 and pays off the Nordstrom's card. He then adds $38.90 to the monthly payment on the QBank card. And the process goes on.

LIST OF DEBTS —John Smith as of December 1, 20XX (year he graduated)					
Creditor/ Purchase	Monthly payment	Balance due	Payment date	Payoff date	Interest rate
Nat'l School Loan	$1,007.94	$95,030.00	3rd	11/3/XX	5%
Simple Auto Fin.	321.00	11,688.85	15th	8/15/XX	11.5%
QBank	168.04 ~~129.14~~	4,304.80	17th	7/17/XX	24%
Nordstrom's	~~38.90~~ ~~18.90~~	~~902.58~~	~~25th~~	~~2/25/XX~~	~~21%~~
Dr. Tabb (dentist)	~~20.00~~	~~60.00~~	~~1st~~	~~2/1/XX~~	~~0%~~
TOTALS	$1,496.98	$111,986.23			

By continuing to roll each of the payments up to the next line, John will ultimately pay the entire $1,496.98 on his school loan. Add to that other instances of God's grace and increases in salary at work. When you implement a plan like this, you'll be amazed at God's faithfulness to help you eliminate all debt.

People often ask why they shouldn't pay their large interest rate debts first. If they did, they might pay all their debt a month or so earlier. However, the encouragement obtained by paying one or more smaller debts first is much more valuable. Paying off debt can feel as if it will go on forever, so we need perseverance. To bolster that perseverance, encouragement makes a huge difference.

Minimum Payments

As you pay down your debt, your minimum credit card payments will shrink each month. At some point, you might be tempted to make only the minimum payment to free up money. Let's look at what happens when you make only the minimum payment on a credit card.

When John started his debt pay-down analysis, his QBank

credit card had a balance of $4,304.80, and his minimum payment is $129.14. The bank will drop the minimum payment each month as the principle due drops. If John makes only the minimum payment each month, it will take him twenty-two and a half years to pay off the QBank card. But if he locks in the payment at $129.14, he'll pay off the card in under five years, and he'll save $5,082.

As the balance drops, so will the required minimum payment. The overall difference is interest on the unpaid balance each month. It's amazing how much difference it can make if we pay attention to how lenders charge interest.

Home Buying

Deferred gratification will help you pay off student debt as quickly as possible. This concept is important in all spending decisions, but especially when it comes to buying a home. You can take smaller steps along the way rather than buying your dream home as soon as you can possibly squeeze in the payment.

Ask yourself whether buying a home is better than renting. *Kiplinger's Magazine*[84] listed advantages of owning a home. The first they listed are the tax advantages. They may include:

• A deduction for mortgage interest and points

• A deduction for property taxes

• Some tax credit for specific improvements (such as residential energy credits)

• Tax-free gain up to a limit upon the sale of a personal residence that has increased in value

The second benefit *Kiplinger's* lists is leverage. Leverage is borrowing the money necessary to buy the house. Leverage is alternatively known as more debt. You should obey God's principles of not being in bondage when a banker touts this advantage. While leverage can benefit a homeowner, it should never be a reason to buy. Leverage can violate God's principles and bring negative consequences.

The third benefit *Kiplinger's* listed is considering the house as a hedge against inflation. But keep in mind that housing prices can go down too. A hedge can quickly become a weight, dragging the unwary homeowner to financial ruin. Over the past decades, many homeowners faced financial ruin because they had purchased too much house so their equity could increase. The markets didn't increase, and the houses were lost, along with down payments and improvement costs.

Going into a home purchase with the idea of leveraging and hedging makes the house an investment. Never consider your home an investment. It is the place where you live. If God blesses you and you get some financial gain while living in it, be thankful.

When looking at houses, ask yourself what you need. Then ask what you can afford. By determining these two factors up front, you can draw a line when pressured to buy more than you can reasonably handle.

Dave Ramsey says that if people buy more house than they can reasonably afford and don't have an emergency fund, Murphy of Murphy's Law will move into their house. In other words, things will break. And without any financial slack in the spending plan, those things either won't get fixed due to lack of funds, or you'll use credit, taking steps backward in your debt pay-down progress.

Take a couple of guidelines into account when looking to buy a house. First, the government agencies Federal National Mortgage Association and Federal Home Loan Mortgage Corp, who buy, repackage, and resell mortgages to investors, have guidelines for mortgage borrowing. They have determined the monthly house payment, or PITI (principal, interest, taxes, and insurance), should equal no more than 28 percent of the borrower's monthly gross income. How does that pencil out?

For a family with a monthly income of $5,000, the Principal, Interest, Taxes, and Insurance (PITI) should not exceed $1,400. Breaking PITI down further, reasonable insurance should be somewhere in the $150 per month range, leaving $1,250 for principal, interest, and taxes. Of principal, interest, and taxes, the property taxes could be anywhere from $150 per month to over $350 per month. Using the low end of $150 leaves $1,100 for a payment.

A thirty-year mortgage with a $1,100 payment at an interest rate of 6 1/4 percent will be a total mortgage borrowed of about $180,000. Assuming 20 percent down, the house purchase price is $225,000. To add to this guideline, FNMA & FHLMC also say total indebtedness, including mortgages, car loans, student loans, credit cards, etc., should not exceed 36 percent of gross income. In the case of the family above, this would leave $700 per month for car loans, school loans, credit card payments, and any other indebtedness.

The *Family Financial Workbook*'s guideline for a family of four in the same income range states housing costs should not exceed 38 percent of net spendable income. Net spendable income is gross income minus tithe and income-related taxes. Let's pencil that out with the same family.

To start the same calculation for the same family with an income of $5,000 a month, we need to calculate the net spendable income. Start with the gross income and subtract estimated taxes of 17.5 percent and giving of 10 percent, which leaves $3,625 for net spendable income. Of the net spendable income, 38 percent is $1,377.50 for housing.

Breaking housing down further, we can once again subtract insurance of $150 per month and property taxes of $150 per month. A good number for house maintenance is an average of

$100 per month, and the utilities, if you're not wasteful and the house is not too big, can be under $100 per month.

Of the $1,377.50, we now have $897.50 for a payment. Using a thirty-year mortgage at about 6 1/4 percent will determine a total initial mortgage of about $125,000. Again assuming 20 percent down, we have a house purchase price of $156,250. The *Family Financial Workbook*[85] is much more conservative, but I suspect few people who follow these guidelines are in trouble with their mortgages.

This doesn't look hopeful, does it? Well, there's major hope in the next few paragraphs. I hope this will be an eye-opener for you. We'll take some time and compare two couples who want to buy their first homes. In the comparison below, you will see how a little-discussed principle can save you tens of thousands or hundreds of thousands of dollars. We've discussed this principle before. It's "deferred gratification," meaning we don't have to have everything right now. We can wait for it until the resources are available.

There's a way to get the home you think is appropriate without spending as much money as the typical homebuyer does. The method is illustrated by the example below. I got this example while teaching the "Your Finances in Changing Times" seminar at churches around the country as a volunteer with Christian Financial Concepts (now Crown Financial Ministries).

Two families want to buy a home: the Biggers and the Smalls. The Biggers are typical homebuyers. They buy more than they think they can afford because the realtor told them it was the right thing to do. The Smalls are disciplined home buyers and use the principle of deferred gratification. Ultimately, they both want the same house. Here's a comparison of the two families and their home-buying adventures.

1. First, they both have $60,000 (20 percent) to put down on a $300,000 house they have decided is perfect.

2. The Biggers go ahead and do so with a thirty-year, 5.6 percent mortgage. Their payments will be $1,378 per month, and the total of the mortgage payments plus the down payment will cost $566,004 over the thirty years.

3. The Smalls decide they can live somewhere smaller for the first part of their young marriage, and they buy a $180,000 house with a 20 percent ($36,000) down payment. They get a seven-year, 4.6 percent mortgage. Their payment is $2,008, and the total of the mortgage payments plus down payment cost of the smaller home will be $228,700 after the seven years are up. They own their house free and clear.

4. But the Smalls don't stop there. They now sell their smaller house and buy the mirror house next door to the Biggers, using the full value of the smaller house for a down payment on the larger house.

5. They again get a seven-year, 4.6 percent mortgage. Their payment is still $2,008, and the total cost of the bigger home will be $397,399 after the fourteen years are up.

6. At fourteen years, the Biggers start to make significant principal payments on their mortgage loan.

7. But again, the Smalls don't stop there. They continue to make their mortgage payments into their own savings and earn 3 percent. At the end of the mortgage, when the Biggers are just paying off their $556,004 house, the Smalls not only own the mirror house next door, debt-free for about 70 percent of the cost the Biggers paid, but they have more than $553,000 in the bank, including the principle and interest earned on the $24,000 they did not use for a down payment thirty years prior.

Amortization facts:

In the beginning of an amortized loan, the principal part of the payments is very small. Of the $1,377.79 paid by the Biggers on the first payment, only $257.79 goes toward the principal. The rest is interest.

Biggers Amortization Schedule				
Month	Principal Balance	Monthly Payment	Interest part of Payment	Principal Part of Payment
0	$240,000.00			
1	$239,742.21	$1,377.79	$1,120.00	$257.79
2	$239,483.22	$1,377.79	$1,118.80	$258.99

As the months progress, the principal payments get larger. At the end of 14 years, the Biggers are now making a principal payment of $560.97. That is still not even half of the total payment.

167	$175,033.16	$1,377.79	$819.43	$558.36
168	$174,472.19	$1,377.79	$816.82	$560.97
169	$173,908.61	$1,377.79	$814.20	$563.59

8. Interest rates may change during the term of the example. Housing prices may fluctuate. But the huge difference can change only so much. These principles work. The only variable is how many tens or hundreds of thousands of dollars they will save.

Some people will pay off their student loans, car loans, and credit cards but decide not to pay off the mortgage. Well-meaning but mistaken financial counselors have told them to keep their mortgages for the tax deduction. Even some highly educated, well-respected financial experts advocate borrowing for deductions. Here's why it doesn't work.

Assume a taxpayer has a monthly payment of $1,000 in deductible mortgage interest. Also, assume they are in the 22 percent federal tax bracket and the 8 percent state tax bracket.

- Being in the 30 percent bracket (federal and state combined), the taxpayer will get back $300 a month in taxes not due at the end of the year because of their mortgage interest payment.
- Picture $1,000 less $300. Wait! The taxpayer's out $700 net per month ($8,400 annually). Less painful than being out $12,000 annually, but here's not the place to stop.
- Assume the taxpayer pays off the mortgage and keeps the $1,000 per month.
- Still being in the 30 percent bracket, the taxpayer's going to owe $300 per month at the end of the year by not paying the tax-deductible interest.
- Now picture $1,000 per month kept less $300 paid in monthly taxes. Wow, the taxpayer still has $700 per month left in their pocket ($8,400 annually).
- Net $8,400 out or net $8,400 kept. Which would you choose?
- Now the next step. Some people hate paying taxes, and the idea of paying $300 a month to the government is repugnant if there's any way to avoid it.
- The taxpayer should pay off the mortgage and give the $1,000 they were paying in interest to their church or a deserving ministry. Then the taxpayer can still get the $300 per month ($3,600 annual) back in tax savings.
- The church or ministry has an additional $12,000 per year to use for their ministries, and the taxpayer has her deduction without the bondage of mortgage debt.

Impulse List

Many people struggle with impulse buying as they form their spending plan. Other than being content with what God has provided, there is no real fix for this. Providentially, a form was developed which has been useful in helping people develop self-control. It's called the Impulse List. You can find it in the Forms and Tools Appendix, in the *Family Financial Workbook*,[86] at www.SayNoToCollegeDebt.com, and below.

The list works like this:

- When you see an item or service you want but is not in your spending plan, promise yourself that, during the next thirty days, you will find at least two more prices on the item before you buy it.

- Write down the item, the store, and the price on the Impulse List, as shown below.

Impulse List

Date	Item	Store/ Price	Store/ Price	Store/ Price
March 1	Bluetooth Beanie Hat	Huge Box $18.97		

- After you have waited at least a week (many don't have to wait a full thirty days), found your prices, decided you still want it, and you've fit it into your spending plan, buy it.

- The nice thing about this method is that, by the time you've thought about the purchase while finding other prices, the impulse will often have passed. At that point, cross the item off the list and keep the list for the next time you get the impulse to buy something you don't need.

Giving

People in debt don't want to think about giving. It's frightening to put money in the offering plate when it seems as if it should go toward the bills.

Although many secular authors approach the idea of giving as a sort of ethereal obligation to humanity, there are good, solid reasons for a Christian to give. And contrary to what you might hear, the main reason is not to fund the church. That's a terrific benefit but not the reason.

The bottom line for giving is obedience and trust. God already has all He needs and doesn't need anything from us. We give so we can see God's trustworthiness. When we give money to God out of obedience (He did tell us to be generous and give), although we could have used it to pay bills or buy something we want or need, we allow Him the opportunity to show us how much He can be trusted. What a joy to find God is dependable and can be trusted to care for us and our needs. See the Scripture Appendix for scriptures on giving.

All too often, we say we trust God but we really don't. As we trust God to provide what we need to make our college-loan payments, He will show us how much we can trust Him. He has promised to care for us, and we need to let Him do what He promised. It's a wonderful way to live, and the relief of pressure will free us up to love our families. We will also be freer to respond when God asks something of us.

In the appendix, I have listed a couple of great books on giving. Please get those and use them to gain understanding of giving according to God's principles.

APPENDICES
Scripture Appendix

The primary sources for these listings are *The Word on Finances*[87] and *The Thompson Chain-Reference Bible*.[88]

Seeking Counsel

Psalm 1:1–5

Proverbs 1:5

Proverbs 9:9

Proverbs 11:14

Proverbs 12:1

Proverbs 12:15

Proverbs 12:17

Proverbs 12:25

Proverbs 13:10

Proverbs 13:18

Proverbs 13:20

Proverbs 14:15

Proverbs 15:22

Proverbs 19:20

Proverbs 20:18

Proverbs 24:6

Proverbs 27:9–10

Ecclesiastes 4:13

Matthew 18:15–17

Romans 14:12

Patience and Delayed Gratification

Psalm 33:20

Psalm 37:7

Psalm 40:1

Proverbs 21:5

Proverbs 27:12

Lamentations 3:25

1 Thessalonians 5:14

Hebrews 10:36

James 1:4

God's Provision

Exodus 16:4

Exodus 16:16

Exodus 17:6

Leviticus 25:19

Deuteronomy 2:7

Deuteronomy 8:18

Joshua 22:8

Joshua 24:13

Psalm 24:1

Psalm 25:12–13

Psalm 37:4

Psalm 37:25

Psalm 112:3

Proverbs 8:18–21

Proverbs 10:22

Mark 6:41

1 Chronicles 29:12–14 Philippians 4:19
Nehemiah 9:21 I Timothy 6:6–8

God's Guidance
Psalm 23 Isaiah 48:17
Psalm 25:9 Luke 1:79
Psalm 32:8 John 16:13
Psalm 73:24

Cosigning
Proverbs 6:1–5 Proverbs 17:18
Proverbs 11:15 Proverbs 22:26–27

Giving
Proverbs 3:9–10 Luke 6:38
Proverbs 11:24–25 Romans 11:34–36
Proverbs 18:16 Romans 12:6,8
Proverbs 22:9 1 Corinthians 13:3
Job 41:11 2 Corinthians 9:6–7
Matthew 5:42 1 Timothy 6:18
Luke 3:11 Hebrews 13:16

Personality and Vocational Testing

In the realm of personality testing, you'll find only a handful of tests doing basically the same thing with some variations but called by different names. Probably the most well-known is the Myers-Briggs Type Indicator (MBTI). You can take the MBTI online or with a counselor or therapist. The online tests are free, but if you have in-depth questions about your results, the personal touch of a counselor or therapist might help.

But free is rarely free. The organization must maintain its website and software, so somewhere in the process, they will get something from you. It may be anonymous data about you, data about you tied to your information, or your contact information. Any of those can lead to unwanted intrusions into your life in the future. Sometimes it's "cheaper" to pay for something up front than to pay with unintended consequences later. Think about the personal data you are divulging before you submit the information.

Another common test is the DISC Assessment. The DISC assessment is available online for free. This test uses word pictures to describe the four primary personality types. DISC stands for Dominant, Influencer, Steady, and Compliant. One version uses animals for the personality picture. "D" is a lion, "I" is an otter, "S" is a golden retriever, and "C" is a beaver. By combining the scores of the four personality types, you'll be identified with one of sixteen basic personality profiles.

The most in-depth of the common personality tests is the Minnesota Multiphasic Personality Inventory. "The Minnesota Multiphasic Personality Inventory (MMPI) is a psychological test that assesses personality traits and psychopathology. It is primarily intended to test people who are suspected of having mental health or other clinical issues."[89] It's available online, but for the purposes of preparing for college, it's probably overkill.

On the other side of the spectrum, we see many free personality tests in magazines and on the internet. As a rule, if you are serious about your college career, you should not take them. Stick to the common, well-established tests and move on from there.

Once you have picked and taken a personality test, move on to career or vocational testing. You can take them through your local community college. Sometimes you don't need to be a student to avail yourself of testing resources.

Looking online, we can find a multitude of tests, many of them free. Keep in mind that free is rarely free. For privacy purposes, you may choose to take the test at a counselor's or therapist's office. The law prohibits them from divulging your information without a court order.

That said, at least one organization has excellent testing and won't misuse your information. Crown Financial Ministries (co-founded by Larry Burkett and Howard Dayton) offers both a personality test and a career test. There are charges for both, but I can recommend both tests and the organization without reservation. Take the individual personality (ID) first and then take the Career Direct. The combination should help you to understand yourself better and make wiser choices as you move into your college or vocational school career.

Books for Further Study

Your Career in Changing Times by Ellis and Burkett
  (also has a companion workbook)

Debt-Free Living by Larry Burkett

Using Your Money Wisely by Larry Burkett

How To Manage Your Money by Larry Burkett

The Family Financial Workbook by Larry Burkett

Your Money Counts by Howard Dayton

Money Management for College Students by Larry Burkett

Master Your Money by Ron Blue

The Total Money Makeover by Dave Ramsey

FORMS AND TOOLS APPENDIX

College Cost and Benefit

This tool can help to quantify the benefit of going to college. Even as you use it, remember there are many more reasons to go to college (or not) beyond the financial aspects. If you don't consider the cost, you might fit into the parable in Luke 14:28–29, "For which of you, desiring to build a tower, does not first sit down and count the cost, whether he has enough to complete it? Otherwise, when he has laid a foundation and is not able to finish, all who see it begin to mock him" (ESV). As we've already shown, the cost of college is substantial. While being mocked for a partially completed building has nothing to do with college costs, begging for more time to pay a loan or make a rent payment might have everything to do with college debt.

To do this analysis, pick a four-year degree you'd like to earn. Remember that some disciplines will require a master's degree. In that case, use six years instead of four. You'll find an example below, and you can get blank forms at www.SayNoToCollege Debt.com.

Next, pick a school. The school website should indicate the cost. If the school is local and you can live at home, exclude the dorm and meal plans. If not, you'll need to include those extra costs. Add all the costs per year for all four years.

Now determine how much you think you could earn working full-time in a non-degreed position in your area. Note that you don't get to spend your whole salary, but only what's left after your employer takes out your taxes. Subtract the cost of living on your own or with a roommate. Chances are, the amount you will earn will be eaten by your costs of living. The costs of living include housing, food, automobile, insurance, any debt payments, entertainment, clothing, savings, medical costs, and other miscellaneous spending. Looking over the next four years, subtract your average annual living costs from your annual average salary (net of taxes) and divide it by 12. Make a note of that number. You will need it.

Add the net earnings for the four years to the cost of college for four years. The sum of those two numbers is what it will cost for you to take four years and go to college. This analysis doesn't take inflation or salary increases into account, since salary increases will probably match inflation of costs. Tuition increases are unpredictable, so this analysis doesn't even try to quantify them.

Now write down the annual salary you'd earn at a good job in your targeted field. Calculate the taxes and subtract those from the income. Divide the resulting number by twelve. Subtract the monthly net income from the non-degreed job you didn't take from the monthly net earnings from the degreed job. This indicates how much more money your degree will earn for you. Divide the monthly increased net earnings into the total cost of going to college. The result will tell you how many months you'll work in your degreed job before you will break even for the time and money spent for college.

According to the example on the next page, the degreed accountant will break even in eleven and a half years. This assumes the accountant is thirty-four years old when he or she breaks even and with about thirty more years of work life. He now makes significantly more than he would have without the degree. It sounds like a good deal. For others, the analysis may not turn out so positively.

College Costs for a 4-year Accounting degree			
NC in-state resident costs			
	Annual	Four years	Per Month
Tuition, Books, Supplies, Room, Board, etc.		$76,048	
Net earnings less costs of living for four years Accounting clerk (net of taxes)	$19,680		
per month			$1,640
less rent	-5,994		
less other costs of living	-11,820		
Net lost earnings		7,464	
Total cost of going to college for four years		$83,512	
Degreed Accountant (net of taxes)	$26,940		
per month			$2,245
Monthly increased earnings from Accounting Clerk to Degreed Accountant			$605
Months to make up the total cost of going to college for four years			138
Years of enhanced salary to make up the total cost of going to college for four years			**11.5**

Monthly Estimated Budget Form

The Monthly Estimated Budget form (pictured on the next page from the *Family Financial Workbook*[90]) is the place to summarize the household's average monthly spending. Many families do not have a clear picture of their income and expenses. They may be vaguely aware of an increase in their credit card debt.

MONTHLY ESTIMATED BUDGET
AS OF _____

Monthly Income
GROSS INCOME PER MONTH:
Salary   _____
Interest   _____
Dividends   _____
Other   _____
Total Gross Income Per Month   ☐

LESS:
1. **Tithe/Giving**   ☐

2. **Tax (Fed, State, FICA)**   ☐

Net Spendable Income   ☐

Monthly Living Expenses
3. **Housing**
Mortgage   _____
Insurance   _____
Taxes   _____
Electricity   _____
Gas   _____
Water   _____
Sanitation   _____
Telephone   _____
Maintenance   _____
Assoc, Dues   _____
Other   _____
Total Housing   ☐

4. **Food**   ☐

5. **Automobile**
Payments   _____
Gas & Oil   _____
Insurance   _____
License/Taxes   _____
Maint/Repair   _____
Replace   _____
Total Automobile   ☐

6. **Insurance**
Life   _____
Medical   _____
Other   _____
Total Insurance   ☐

7. **Debts**
Credit Cards   _____
Loans & Notes   _____
Other   _____
Total Debts   ☐

8. **Entertainment & Recreation**
Eating Out   _____
Baby Sitters   _____
Activities/Trips _____
Vacation   _____
Other   _____
Total Entertain & Recreation   ☐

9. **Clothing**   ☐

10. **Savings**   ☐

11. **Medical Expenses**
Doctor   _____
Dentist
Prescriptions   _____
Other   _____
Total Medical Expenses   ☐

12. **Miscellaneous**
Cosmetics
Beauty, Barber _____
Laundry, Clean _____
Allowances   _____
Pets   _____
Subscriptions   _____
Gifts   _____
Christmas Gifts _____
Other   _____
Total Miscellaneous   ☐

13. **Investments**   ☐

14. **School / Child Care**
Tuition
Materials   _____
Transportation _____
Day Care   _____
Total School / Child Care   ☐

TOTAL LIVING EXPENSES   ☐

Income Versus Living Expenses

Net Spendable Income
Less   ☐

Total Living Expenses   ☐

Surplus or Deficit   ☐

113

Completing this form can be painful, since it brings reality into focus. Ignoring reality and continuing out-of-control financial habits, however, is ultimately much more painful.

If you create a spending plan or fill out the Monthly Estimated Budget Form without first tracking all spending for a month, you'll feel discouraged and confused because you merely guessed at the numbers. Before you think about putting numbers on the form, look at your past four credit card statements, your checkbook register, cash-spending records, and any other financial records that show money coming into and going out of your household. Without accurate numbers to start with, the completed form will be useless as a tool for creating and controlling your spending plan.

In this process, recognize that some spending is irregular. Although irregular expenses may not show up as you look through your records, they are part of a real household spending plan. These include annual life insurance payments, semi-annual car insurance payments, periodic teeth cleaning, Christmas and other gifts, and vacations. To account for these important spending items, estimate annual costs for each type of spending and divide by twelve. Then add these figures into the Monthly Estimated Budget form.

This form usually does not balance at first. Don't let this deter you. The pages below the Monthly Estimated Budget form will help you make decisions about what category each spending item should go into. The rest of the spending plan system below is built on those suggested categorizations. You can also find the Excel forms used in the examples below at www.SayNoToCollege Debt.com. The advantage of using the downloaded forms is that much of the arithmetic work is done for you (subtotals and totals) on those forms. The workbook cells that contain formulas have a green background on the downloaded form. You shouldn't change the formulas in any cell that has a green background.

How to Complete
the Monthly Estimated Budget Form

Before you read the detailed instructions below, I suggest watching the videos at www.SayNoToCollegeDebt.com. They will show a new graduate with debt how to put together and administer a spending plan. The videos use numbers new graduates might use, but you can use the same process with your own numbers.

Enter all regular monthly income in the Gross Income per Month section. The lines on the form are common income sources. If you have other dependable monthly income, enter it on the "Other" line. Be sure to make it a monthly number. For annual income, divide the annual number by twelve, and enter it. For quarterly income, divide the quarterly number by three and enter it. If you get paid every other week, multiply your bi-weekly pay by twenty-six and divide it by twelve. If your income varies, estimate your annual income and divide it by twelve. If you use the "other" line, make a note in the white space, naming the income source.

If you use a manual form, total the four lines under Gross Income Per Month. Enter the total in the box to the immediate right. If you use the downloaded form, the green workbook cell will automatically add it for you. Keep in mind that if you use lines or columns other than the ones labeled, the number will not be added to the total in the green box. If any of the formulas get deleted or accidentally changed, download the form again and start over.

Add up your annual giving to your church, ministries, charities, and others. Divide this number by twelve and enter it into the box to the right of "Tithe/Giving." Add up your annual tax payments (federal income tax withheld, state income tax withheld, federal and state income tax underpayments, Medicare tax, FICA tax, state disability, and any other payroll taxes). Divide the sum by twelve and enter that number into the box to the right of "Tax (Fed, State, FICA)."

If you use a manual form, subtract both the monthly Tithe/Giving and the monthly Tax number from the monthly Total Gross income number and enter the result into the Net Spendable Income box. If you use the downloaded form, a formula in the Net Spendable Income cell will do this for you. This number is the amount of money available to run your house and your life every month.

The next category is Housing. The housing category includes all the costs of a home. It includes rent or mortgage payments, insurance on the home or the contents of an apartment, utilities, a telephone, maintenance costs, and other items on the Category listings below. Remember that things like homeowners or renter's insurance are usually semi-annual payments, but the number to enter on this form is a monthly amount. Divide a semi-annual payment by six to get the monthly number. If you use a manual form, add all the numbers on the lines in this category. Then enter the result into the Total Housing box. If you use the downloaded form, the formula in the Total Housing cell will do that for you.

The next category is Food. The food category usually includes all the normal items you buy each month at the grocery store. Enter the number into the box to the right of Food.

The next category is Automobile(s). The automobile category includes all the costs of owning, maintaining, and driving your car or cars. It includes payments, insurance on the car or cars, maintenance costs, registration. If you don't have a payment, this category includes money set aside to replace your car in the future. Remember that things like insurance usually have semi-annual payments, but the number to enter on this form is the monthly amount. Divide a semi-annual payment by six to get a monthly amount. If you use a manual form, add all the numbers on the lines in this category. Then enter the result into the Total Automobile box. If you use the downloaded form, the formula in the Total Automobile cell will do that for you.

If you have medical, dental, life, disability, or liability insurance, figure the monthly cost as you did with other insurances. Enter and total them as you did in the former categories. We already captured car, homeowners, and rental insurance in previous categories, so don't enter them again. If you use a manual form, add all the numbers entered on the lines in this category. Then enter the result into the Total Insurance box. If you use the downloaded form, the formula in the Total Insurance cell will do that for you.

The next category is Debts. The debt category is all the debt payments for credit cards, loans, student loans, and personal loans. The only items that don't belong here are home mortgages, home equity lines of credit (both of which belong in the Housing category), automobile loans (which belong in the Automobile category), and vacation loans. Vacation loans could be timeshare payments, vacation-home payments, boat payments, RV payments, trailer payments, and the like. These all belong in the Entertainment & Recreation category. If you use a manual form, add all the numbers entered on the lines in this category. Then enter the result into the Total Debt box. If you use the downloaded form, the formula in the Total Debt cell will do that for you.

The Entertainment and Recreation category is at the top of the next column. Entertainment and recreation includes vacations, loan payments on the items listed in the prior paragraph, and other items on the form or in the category listing below. Eating out is one of the more difficult expenses to control, and it belongs in this category. If you use a manual form, add all the numbers entered on the lines in this category. Then enter the result into the Total

Entertainment & Recreation box. If you use the downloaded form, the formula in the Total Entertainment & Recreation cell will do that for you.

The clothing category is self-explanatory. However, you don't buy clothing regularly. Set an amount in your spending plan and then spend more or less during different months of the year. Enter the appropriate number into the box or workbook cell.

The best way to handle savings is to make it automatic. David Bach said in his book *The Automatic Millionaire*, "The one way to create lasting financial change that will help you build real wealth over time is to make your financial plan automatic."[91] Do this by arranging for your bank to transfer funds automatically from your paycheck or checking account into your savings account every month. Proverbs 13:11 says that "whoever gathers money little by little makes it grow." Even a little bit per month helps.

Medical expenses consist of all medical costs except insurance, including expenses not covered by your medical insurance. If you use a manual form, add all the numbers entered on the lines in this category. Then enter the result into the Total Medical Expenses box. If you use the downloaded form, a formula in the Total Medical Expenses cell will do that for you.

Miscellaneous consists of anything in the spending plan that doesn't belong somewhere else. As you can see on the form, miscellaneous includes Christmas and other gifts (annual totals divided by twelve), books, magazines, personal grooming, makeup, money spent on pets, and other spending that doesn't belong anywhere else. If you use a manual form, add all the numbers entered on the lines in this category. Then enter the result into the Total Miscellaneous box. If you use the downloaded form, a formula in the Total Miscellaneous cell will do that for you.

Your company will typically deduct your Investments savings from your paycheck. Remember how much a little bit per month can help. Put that amount (monthly average) in the box on the form or in the workbook cell.

The final category is School/Child Care. This category is designed for parents, but students of any age can use it. I used this category for my graduate studies. If your children are in a private school or need after-school care, those amounts go here. This situation can be a blessing to your children but a spending-plan disaster. Enter the numbers on the form and total the category (manually, or let the workbook do it).

The last number to enter on this form is for those who use the manual version. Add up the totals from categories 3–14 and enter the total into the box labeled Total Living Expenses. Be sure to add only categories 3–14, as you have already subtracted categories 1 and 2 from your gross income, and you don't want to double dip. Then copy the Net Spendable Income number (at the top of the left column) into the Net Spendable Income box (just below). Enter the Total Living Expenses, which you just calculated, into the Total Living Expenses box just below. Subtract the latter from the former, and you have your surplus or deficit.

Before you jump to conclusions, be sure you have used only monthly numbers in all your categories and that you've done all the arithmetic correctly. Check with your husband or wife about things you might have been missed. Be sure you haven't forgotten anything or entered anything twice (like auto insurance in both the Automobile category and the Insurance category).

If you have a surplus, that's great. If it's a large surplus, you should make extra payments on your debt or allocate more to savings. You are in an enviable position and should pray and ask God how He wants you to handle the extra He has provided. He has a reason, and you should seek it out.

If you have a deficit (like most of us), you need to figure out how to bring your spending plan into balance. We'll use the next form to do so. That is right after the listing of what income/spending items go into which category.

What Income/Spending Items Go Into Which Category?

Below you'll find suggestions for putting specific spending into the correct category. These are taken from the *Biblical Perspectives on Money* workbook[92] and have been slightly modified for this usage. The list below will help you understand the Budget Categories that were used to design the Budget Guidelines in the Budget Analysis form below.

Gross Income Per Month: This category captures all income, whether taxable or not, including items such as child support or inheritance money received. Estimate any irregular or lump-sum income; a prior year's tax return may help you estimate. Convert all numbers in this category to monthly amounts by dividing the annual totals by twelve. Make sure to enter gross monthly earnings before any payroll deductions.

Category 1 Tithe/Giving: This category captures all giving to the church, Christian ministries, and other charitable organizations (Red Cross, Boys and Girls Club, etc.).

Category 2 Taxes: Include federal withholding, Social Security, and state and local taxes. Self-employed individuals should use this category to set aside money for quarterly estimated tax payments. Beware of the tendency to treat unpaid tax money as a windfall profit.

Other Payroll Deductions: Include deductions for insurance, savings or debt payments, bonds, stock programs, retirement, and union dues in gross income and deduct them in their proper categories (Insurance, Savings, Debt, Investments, Miscellaneous). Recording those payments in their proper categories provides a more comprehensive picture of where the money is being spent and aligns more accurately with the guideline spending plan percentages found in the Budget Analysis form instructions.

Net Spendable Income: (Gross Income minus Tithe/Giving and Taxes) is the portion available for family spending. Please note that "Net Pay" on a pay stub is not the same as "Net Spendable Income."

Category 3 Housing Expenses: This category includes all monthly expenses necessary to operate the home, including rent or mortgage payments, taxes, insurance, maintenance, and utilities. The amount used for utility payments should be an average monthly amount, which can be obtained by calling the utility providing the service. If renting, be sure to secure renter's insurance. If you are unable to pinpoint the exact amounts you have spent for maintenance, use five percent of the monthly mortgage payment.

Category 4 Food Expenses: This category is for all monthly grocery expenses, including paper goods and nonfood products you normally purchase at grocery stores. Make sure to include any similar items you buy at convenience stores or warehouse clubs. Do not include restaurants or fast food purchased and eaten away from home. You'll track those expenses in Category 8: Entertainment & Recreation.

Category 5 Automobile Expenses: All monthly expenses of operating a car, including payments, insurance, gas, oil, maintenance, and money set aside to purchase the next car are included here. Divide the total annual maintenance spending by twelve to estimate the monthly expense. Set aside the monthly portion of any annual or semi-annual auto insurance payments monthly to avoid a future cash crisis.

Category 6: Insurance: This includes health, life, disability, long-term care, and other insurances, but not those associated with the home, vacation homes, automobiles, or recreation vehicles.

Category 7: Debts: This category does not include your home mortgage or automobile payments, but it does include all other monthly payments required to meet past debt obligations, including payments to family or friends. Monthly payments for old credit card debt belong here. If you use a credit card for current expenses, however, each of those uses should be captured in the appropriate category. Pay the total bill for those amounts when the bill comes, along with whatever monthly payment you already make, to reduce the old debt on that card. Better yet—pay current expenses with a check or debit card.

Category 8: Entertainment & Recreation: Include vacation savings, camping trips, sporting equipment, hobby expenses, and athletic events. Don't forget eating out, babysitting, and lunches purchased away from home. Control this category easier by using cash instead of credit cards. This category includes all the annual costs (including payments and insurance) of a vacation home, a boat, ownership in a timeshare, or other vacation expenses.

Category 9: Clothing: Since many people often use credit cards to buy clothing, prior clothing costs are often buried in debt payments. Try to determine an annual amount and divide it by twelve.

Category 10: Savings: Every family should allocate something for savings. Not only does a savings account provide funds for emergencies, but it is also a key element in good planning and financial freedom. Keep these funds in an easily accessible place, such as a savings account or money market account with check privileges and no penalties for early withdrawal. Don't confuse this category with funds allocated for investing, even though we sometimes refer to investing as retirement savings or college savings.

Category 11: Medical/Dental Expenses: This includes insurance deductibles, doctors' bills, eyeglasses, prescriptions, counseling fees, orthodontist visits, etc. Use a yearly average divided by twelve to determine a monthly amount. List health insurance premiums in Category 6: Insurance.

Category 12: Miscellaneous: Include expenses that do not fit anywhere else: pocket allowance (coffee money), Christmas and other gifts, toiletries, and haircuts. Many people underestimate miscellaneous spending. To get a clear picture of your spending habits in this category, you will need to monitor it carefully for at least two months. Self-discipline is the key to controlling miscellaneous spending. This category is another good candidate for using cash only. Create a list of specifics you'll pay from this category to keep it from becoming the leak that never stops flowing.

Category 13: Investments: This category is for long-term investing, retirement, or college savings. Regular savings (building an emergency reserve) is captured in Category 10: Savings. When you achieve debt-free status, you can divert more money to this category.

Category 14: School/childcare: Use this category for expenses associated with children and school activities, including the cost of childcare. (Important Note: This is an optional category. The Percentage Guideline Schedules allocate 100 percent of income before considering this category. Any funds allocated to this category must be trimmed from other spending-plan categories to keep the spending plan balanced. Make sure to reduce other categories to make up for any percentage of your income you allocate here.)

While I cover the Budget Analysis form next, it ties in closely with the Debt List (covered immediately after the Budget Analysis form). It will be easier to create them both at the same time. Some changes might affect both forms, so creating them together could help you keep track of this fairly complicated process.

Budget Analysis Form

The Budget Analysis form (partially pictured below from the *Family Financial Workbook*[93]) assists you in making the tough decisions required to spend equal to or less than you make. Spending less than you make is the only way to move toward financial freedom, including achieving debt-free status. This form is the response to the jarring realization that you spend more than you bring in. As I've said, overspending results in eroding savings or other assets, increasing debt, or both. We'll look at the category totals, but we also need to pay attention to the source numbers that make up the category totals.

BUDGET ANALYSIS FORM				
Income per year _____				
Income per month _____				
Monthly payment category	Existing budget	Guideline budget	Difference + or −	New Monthly budget
1. Tithe/giving				
2. Tax				
Net spendable income				
3. Housing				
4. Food				
5. Auto				
6. Insurance				
7. Debts				
8. Entertain & Recreation				
9. Clothing				
10. Savings				
11. Medical				

How to Complete the Budget Analysis Form

Before you read the detailed instructions below, please watch the videos at www.SayNoToCollegeDebt.com. They'll show a new, indebted graduate how to put together and administer a spending plan. Then you can go through the same process, using your own numbers to make the system work.

To complete the Budget Analysis form, you need a printout of the recently completed Monthly Estimated Budget. Round your numbers to the nearest dollar. Getting too detailed can lead to frustration, and then we're tempted throw all the work into a desk drawer and forget about it. At least until the lack of plan results in financial disaster, and the results of financial disaster. Keep in mind that one of the most painful and common results of financial disaster is the breakup of marriages and families. Isn't a marriage and family worth the effort it takes to deal with this process and the uncomfortable realities and decisions?

To get started, enter your monthly income at the top of the form. Multiply that number by twelve and enter the result onto the Income Per Year line. Then enter the spending category totals from the Monthly Estimated Budget Form into the column labeled Existing Budget. If you use a manual form, copy all the numbers for this column, including the totals, from the Monthly Estimated Budget Form. If you downloaded the form from www.SayNoTo CollegeDebt.com, you won't need to fill in your the Income per Year. It has a green background and contains a formula. The workbook will also input your net spendable income, total living expenses, and difference.

If you see very small differences between the totals on the two forms, chalk that up to rounding. If you see large differences between the totals on the two forms, recheck your data entry and any calculations you may have completed outside the Excel forms. Find those errors and fix them. There's no point in completing a spending plan process and finding out your beginning data is wrong.

Next, go to the Crown Financial Ministries website (www.Crown.org) to find your appropriate percentage guidelines for the Guideline Budget column. Use the term "spending guides" in the search function and select spending guides from the options provided. At the time of this writing, the spending guides on the Crown site encompass families made up of single with roommate, single without roommate, single parent, family of two, family of four, and family of six. Choose the one that most closely resembles your situation, download the PDF file, and print it.

On the PDF printout, select the income range that is closest to your annual income. When near the middle between two Gross Household Income numbers, select the higher of the two. Circle or highlight the selected column on your printout for ease of reference.

At this point, multiply the Income Per Month times the percentage on the Tithe/Giving line in the column you selected and enter the number into the box on the Tithe/Giving line under Guideline Budget. Next, multiply the Income per Month times the percentage on the Total Taxes line in the column you selected and enter the number into the box on the Tax line under Guideline Budget. If you use the Excel form, enter those numbers into the appropriate workbook cells. If doing this manually, subtract the numbers in the Guideline Budget column for categories 1 and 2 from the Income Per Month and enter the remainder into the Net Spendable Income box in the Guideline Budget column. In the Excel workbook, this will happen automatically. Before you throw your hands up and quit, please know this column has the most complicated calculations in the whole process. You'll soon have hard decisions to make, but they won't be technical.

Moving on to the box in the Budget Guidelines column for the Housing category, multiple the **Net Spendable Income** times the percentage on the Housing line in the income column you have selected. Please note that you are not multiplying the Income Per Month now, but the Net Spendable Income. That will be true for the rest of the categories below (categories 4–14).

Now go to the box in the Budget Guidelines column for the Food category and multiply the Net Spendable Income times the percentage on the Food line in the income column you have selected. Fill in the rest of the column through category 14 in the same manner. If you have no School/Childcare spending, put a zero in the School/Childcare box. If you use the manual form, add the numbers in the column for categories 3–14 and put that number into the box in the column on the Total Living Expenses line. Then subtract the Total Living Expenses Line from the Net Spendable Income line and enter the remainder into the Difference box in this column.

There are two reasons why you may have a number in the Difference box. First, if you entered a number in School/Childcare, the total will be thrown off. We'll address that when discussing the New Monthly Budget column. If not, it may just be a rounding issue. If you put nothing in the School/Childcare box and the Difference number is less than ten dollars, move on to the next step. If there is nothing in the School/Childcare box and rounding is more than ten dollars, you have an error in the column, so you'll need to find it and fix it. Go back through the instructions and reenter the numbers. If you have a number in the School/Childcare box, rounding could cause the number in the Difference box to be within ten dollars of that number, but not exactly the number. If not, there is an error, so you'll need to find it and fix it. The same rounding rules hold for the Difference number if you are using the Excel workbook.

The Difference column is next. If you use the Excel workbook, that whole column is calculated automatically, so you can move on to the next step. If you use the manual method, follow these instructions. For each line (category), subtract the number in the Guideline Budget box from the number in the Existing Budget box and enter the difference into the Difference column on the appropriate line. Do this all the way down the column.

Now comes the hard part. It's time to bring the out-of-balance budget into balance. Before starting this next step, understand that the guideline budget is just a guideline. It is not a hard, fast rule you need to follow. It is provided to help you see where the possibility for change exists. If there is a good reason to vary from the guideline number, then you should vary from the guideline number.

Starting with the largest number in the difference column, either positive or negative, look for places to cut spending. The largest difference numbers usually have the largest potential for change. The goal is to fill out the New Monthly Budget column with realistic numbers that show the Net Spendable Income equal to the Total Living Expenses with a difference of zero. Work on that until you achieve your goal.

A discussion of the changes that can be made is beyond the scope of this book, but you can pick up some of the titles listed in the Books for Further Study appendix. This is also an important time for prayer. I believe God is capable of providing a way for you to balance your spending plan and get out of the bondage of debt. Seek His wisdom and guidance. James 1:5 tells us, "If any of you lacks wisdom, you should ask God, who gives generously to all without finding fault, and it will be given to you." Take God up on that promise.

Once you have balanced your spending plan, make another Monthly Estimated Budget Form, using the changes you've made. You'll use the new copy as you work on controlling the spending plan.

Debt List Form

Use the Debt List Form (pictured below from the *Family Financial Workbook*[94]) to list all your debts. It is a snapshot of your indebtedness at the time you start your spending plan process. This short explanation will explain how to complete the form, but you can find a video of the whole debt pay-down process at www.SayNoToCollegeDebt.com. The video first shows how to complete the form and then shows how to use it to pay down your debt.

LIST OF DEBTS AS OF _____						
Creditor/ Purchase	Monthly payments	Balance due	Payment date	Payoff date	Interest rate	Payments past due

How to Complete the Debt List Form

As with the Monthly Estimated Budget Form process, start by gathering data. First, collect payment coupons for every one of your debts. Even though a mortgage or a car payment doesn't belong in the Debt category in the spending plan system, they do need to be on this form. You should also include any personal loans from friends or family or single-payment loans from a bank or credit union. Nothing is more frustrating than getting well into a spending-plan process and finding that you left a debt off the list. That can tempt you to abandon your plan.

With the data gathered and using the form below, enter each of your debts. As with the other forms, you can find the Debt List at www.SayNoToCollegeDebt.com in an Excel format. The only difference between the manual form and the Excel form is that the Excel form automatically totals the columns for Monthly Payments and Balance Due. For easy use of the debt pay-down plan in the video, list the debts in order of outstanding balance, with the largest balance due at the top. For most families, the largest balance due would be their home mortgage. For a student just coming out of school with student loans, the largest balance will probably be a student loan.

In the first column, enter the name of the creditor and, if needed for reference, what was purchased. In the second column, enter the monthly payment. For mortgages, car loans, and other loans with fixed payments, enter the fixed payment amount. For credit cards, enter the current minimum payment due, even if you have been paying more than the minimum. In the third column, put the balance due. Some payment coupons can be confusing, so be sure to enter the balance due now, not the balance due before you made the last payment. To make sure you make your payments, enter the day of the month when your payment is normally due. You don't need the month, just the day.

This next column can be tricky. If you have a fully amortized loan, like a mortgage or a car loan, your bank can tell you the payoff date. If you have a fixed payment loan of any type (including a student loan), the loan servicing company can tell you the payoff date. If you have credit card debt, look at your statement or payment coupon to see how many months of payments remain if you make only the minimum payments. Add that many months to the current date and use that date. Don't merely divide the balance by the payment amount.

Finally, enter the interest rate, as shown on your payment coupon or loan documents. Banks, credit unions, loan servicers, and credit card companies can also tell you the interest rate on your loan or card. I hope you don't ever need to use the final column. Penalties and extra interest incurred by past-due payments can devastate a tight spending plan.

Once you've entered all the numbers, total the Monthly Payments and Balance Due columns. And be aware that the Monthly Payments total will probably not equal the spending in the Debt category. Remember that mortgage payments, car payments, and vacation home/RV/boat payments are not captured in the Debt section, but in Housing, Auto, and Entertainment/ Recreation categories. The Debt List/Debt Pay-down Plan video at www.SayNoToCollegeDebt.com explains further how to use this form to effectively pay off all these debts.

Monthly Budget Workbook

The Monthly Budget Worksheet (pictured on the next page from the *Biblical Perspectives on Money* workbook[95]) is used to record your income and spending so you can control your spending rather than your spending controlling you.

How to Complete the Monthly Budget Worksheet

Like the other forms, the Monthly Budget Worksheet is available at www.SayNoToCollegeDebt.com in an Excel format. The Excel version does handy subtotals and totals for the process. You can do the process described below daily, but I recommend weekly. It shouldn't take more than an hour per week. Can you dedicate one hour a week to getting your spending under control? It's well worth it.

The form shown below is too small to use, so if you're not going to use the Excel version, you can download it and print the download to use manually. If you use the manual version, enter the monthly spending plan numbers from the New Budget column of your completed Budget Analysis Form into the boxes on the Budgeted Amount line near the top of the form. The Income box should be a positive number, and all the spending should be negative numbers. Put the appropriate numbers into the appropriate columns, starting with the planned Income on the left, followed by the planned Tithe/Giving in the next column, followed by the Taxes in the next column, and so on until you've filled in the entire line. Enter a zero if you don't plan to spend in that category. It's a good idea to check your data entry by adding the positive and negative numbers across that line. The result should be zero, as on your Budget Analysis Form.

As you start your spending plan, you may have to add the habit of keeping all your credit and debit card receipts, using du-

Monthly Budget Worksheet
Month of _____

Category>	Income	1. Tithe/Giv.	2. Taxes	3. Housing	4. Food	5. Auto	6. Insur	7. Debt	8. Ent/Rec	9. Clothing	10. Savings	11. Medical	12. Misc	13. Invest	14. Sch/Child
Budgeted Amount>	$	$	$	$	$	$	$	$	$	$	$	$	$	$	$
Day of Month															
1															
2															
3															
4															
5															
6															
7															
8															
9															
10															
11															
12															
13															
14															
15															
MTD Subtotal															
16															
17															
18															
19															
20															
21															
22															
23															
24															
25															
26															
27															
28															
29															
30															
31															
Month Total															
Surplus/Def															
YTD Budget															
YTD Total Actl															
YTD Surpl/Def															

Budget Summary

This Month
Total Income $ _____
Minus Total Spending $ _____
Equals Surplus/Deficit $ _____

+

Prior Year-To-Date
Total Income $ _____
Minus Total Spending $ _____
Equals Surplus/Deficit $ _____

=

Year-To-Date
Total Income $ _____
Minus Total Spending $ _____
Equals Surplus/Deficit $ _____

134

plicate checks, and writing down anything you buy with cash. Without all the records available to enter into the form, your tracking will not be accurate. Without accurate tracking, the system will break down, and you will have a nasty surprise when the money runs out before the month ends. It's a matter of discipline. One suggestion that has worked for me is to carry a small notebook and pencil to write down any spending for which you do not get a receipt. I've also been known to use my phone to snap a picture of the fuel pump when the receipt dispenser is not working.

When your first chosen day to enter your spending comes around, sort your receipts by date. If your first spending was $1.15 in cash, paid for a donut on the way to work on the 2nd of the month, you enter -$1 into the box on the line for the 2nd of the month in the Entertainment/Recreation column. If you wonder why that is Entertainment, revisit the list above, showing what spending goes into what category. On the 3rd, you wrote a check for a car payment of $323.56. Enter -$324 into the box in the Auto category on the line for the 3rd. That same day, you used your debit or credit card to spend $67.45 on groceries. Enter -$67 into the box on the same line, but in the column for the Food category. These are easy entries.

On the 5th, you got paid. The payroll entry is typically a compound entry, so let's walk through it. Your gross pay for the prior two weeks was $2,000. From that gross amount, your company took out $250.40 for your withheld taxes, $45.24 for your portion of your medical insurance, and $30 for your contribution to the company's 401(k). That leaves a check of $1,674.36. To enter this, on the line for the 5th, you enter $2,000 in the Income column, -$240.40 in the Taxes column, -$45.24 in the Insurance column, and -$30.00 in the Investments column. On the 6th, you got $50 from your grandmother, who never can figure out what to buy you for your birthday. Enter it on the line for the 6th in the Income column. The 6th is also the day you enter spending, so that is the day you write your check for Tithe/Giving. Since everything we receive is from God, no matter what the source, you base your giving on the $2,050 you received. And as you probably don't want to elevate the government above God, you do your giving on the gross income, not on what's left after the government takes its share.

Enter everything else you've spent or brought in the same way during each scheduled recordkeeping day. When in doubt about where you should record something, use the list above to see what goes in each category.

When you get to the 15th, you'll see a line. That is to remind you that you can subtotal all the income and spending through the 15th. There is nothing magic about this line; it's there only to add all the contents of each column on the fifteen lines above. If you use the Excel workbook, it does this for you automatically. If you do this manually, you can add the columns and put the numbers in the appropriate columns on that line. This line will provide a mid-point view of your spending for the month. If you get to Entertainment/Recreation and see that you have already spent 80 percent of your eating-out money, you should spend less for the rest of the month so you won't overspend that category. If you are under, you can look to spend a little more or keep up the good discipline and not spend as much that month so you can put extra toward your debt.

After the end of the month, when you've recorded all your spending and income, you will need to fill out the bottom five lines of the schedule and the three boxes below the schedule. Assuming you did your subtotal on the 15th, total each column from the subtotal down. The spending or income from the first fifteen days is already on the subtotal line. If you didn't do the subtotal line, add the income/spending for each column for the whole month, and enter each column's result on the line labeled Month Total in the appropriate column. The Excel workbook contains formulas to make this happen automatically.

For each column on the next line (Surplus/Def), subtract the number on the Month Total line from the number on the Budgeted Amount line. Pay attention to minuses and plusses. This line shows whether your income was more or less than planned. It also shows overspending or underspending for the month. For the first few months, these will probably be larger than you would like. As you refine the process, they will get smaller.

On the next line down, enter the Budgeted Amount times the number of months into the spending-plan year. It is titled YTD Budget. Most people run their spending plans on a calendar year, so January would be the first month, and the numbers on this line would be the Budgeted Amount for each column times one. In March, it would be the Budgeted Amount for each column times three. For August, it would be times eight, and for December, it would be times twelve.

The next line is the year-to-date accumulation of income and spending. It is titled YTD Total Actl (For Year-To-Date Total Actual). To calculate each column on this line, add the number from the same box from the prior month's worksheet to the Month Total for the present month. If this is the first month of the Spending Plan year, this line is the same as the Month Total line.

For the next line, subtract the YTD Total Actl from the YTD Budget for each column. This line shows your year-to-date income and spending against your year-to-date spending plan.

Finally, you'll see three summary boxes at the bottom of the worksheet. They provide a higher-level look at how your spending plan is working. To complete them, copy the number from the Month Total box in the Income column to the top line of the first box (labeled Total Income). Copy the number from the YTD Total Actl box in the Income column to the Total Income line, on the third box. The Total Income for the middle box should be the YTD Total Actl from the prior month's Monthly Budget Workbook.

For the next line down for all three boxes, total all the boxes on the Month Total line except Income, and put it on the first box's Minus Total Spending line. Then, total all the boxes on the YTD Total Act line except Income, and put it on the third box's Minus Total Spending Line. Then, total all the boxes on the YTD Total Act line from the prior month except Income, and put it on the middle box's Minus Total Spending line. Subtract each of the Total Income numbers from their corresponding Minus Total Spending numbers and enter the difference on the Equals Surplus/Deficit line in each box. These boxes are all calculated automatically on the Excel workbook.

The numbers on the YTD Surplus/Deficit line show whether the income or spending is in line with the spending plan. The bottom-line numbers in the Budget Summary boxes show how the spending plan has been working relating to cash in and out. Use both sets of numbers to make adjustments to your spending habits.

Impulse List

Use the Impulse List (pictured below from the *Family Financial Workbook*[96]) to record items you might otherwise have

Impulse List				
Date	Item	Store/ Price	Store/ Price	Store/ Price

purchased on an impulse. It is another tool to help you control your spending rather than letting your spending control you.

How to Complete the Impulse List

The impulse list can take many forms. The one above was suggested by financial author and teacher Larry Burkett. You can use this form, carry a small notebook, or use a note on your smartphone/tablet. As you work your spending plan, you'll want a place to record your spending in cash or to record other financial data anyway. Adding an impulse list would be an easy step.

Any version of this form works. When you want to buy something that is not in your spending plan, make note of the date, the item, the cost, and where you found it. During the next thirty days, promise yourself to find at least two more prices for comparison purposes. Make a note of the two other prices and where you found them.

At the end of thirty days, you'll know where to get the best price, and one of two things will happen. The best result is that by taking a little time to think, you decide you don't need the item. Or you still want it, and you've probably figured a way to fit it into your spending plan. In that case, go ahead and buy it.

ENDNOTES

[i] Out of High School, Into Real Life https://www.nytimes.com/2017/06/23/us/out-of-high-school-into-real-life.html

[ii] G. W. Carver Letter to Booker T. Washington, 1896

[1] https://www.thealternativedaily.com/disadvantages-of-going-to-college/

[2] http://www.ncaa.org/about/resources/research/estimated-probability-competing-professional-athletics

[3] https://work.chron.com/likelihood-someone-becoming-professional-sports-player-26110.html

[4] Ibid

[5] Peterson, E. H. 1963. *The Message Bible.* Carol Stream: Navpress.

[6] Foster, Richard J. 2010. *Freedom of Simplicity: Revised Edition: Finding Harmony in a Complex World.* New York: HarperCollins. Kindle.

[7] Federal Reserve Bank of New York using U.S. Census Bureau statistics (*Fiscal Times* 7/5/2017) http://www.thefiscaltimes.com/2017/07/05/ Value-College-Degree-One-Simple-Chart

[8] CNN Money Average college degree pays off by age 34 (1/9/217) http://money.cnn.com/2017/01/09/pf/college/college-degree-payoff/ index.html

[9] https://stories.starbucks.com/press/2015/starbucks-college-achievement-plan-frequently-asked-questions/

[10] Foster, Richard J. *Freedom of Simplicity: Revised Edition: Finding Harmony in a Complex World* (Kindle Locations 2259-2261). HarperCollins. Kindle Edition.

[11] Holiday, R. (2017, April 3). EntreLeadership [Audio podcast]. Retrieved from https://www.entreleadership.com/blog/podcast

[12] Baldwin, David, https://www.quora.com/What-is-the-purpose-of-high-school

[13] Burkett, L. 1998. *Money Management for College Students.* Chicago: Moody

[14] Ibid

[15] Olasky, M. (2018, September 18). The world and everything in it [audio podcast]. Retrieved from https://worldandeverything.org/

[16] Trade Schools, Colleges & Universities https://www.trade-schools.net/

[17] https://www.theclassroom.com/benefits-going-fouryear-college-11325.html

[18] Stonestreet, J. (2019, July 5). The world and everything in it [audio podcast]. Retrieved from https://worldandeverything.org/

[19] James Hudson Taylor Quotes https://www.goodreads.com/author/quotes/4693730.James_Hudson_Taylor

[20] Anonymous for privacy reasons (email, February 4, 2019)

[21] Ben Kaplan Shares Tips for Scoring College Scholarships https://www.modernmom.com/d97e2114-3a2b-11e3-88b0-bc764e04a41e.html

[22] Staff. 2017. "50 Best Workplaces." *Inc. Magazine*, June 2017.

[23] Staff. 2017. "Building and Keeping an Innovative Workforce." *Inc. Magazine*. September 2017.

[24] https://stories.starbucks.com/press/2015/starbucks-college-achievement-plan-frequently-asked-questions/

[25] https://www.usnews.com/news/blogs/data-mine/2014/10/07/student-loan-expectations-myth-vs-reality

[26] https://www.campusexplorer.com/college-advice-tips/E66537B4/Costs-Of-A-Bachelor-s-Degree-Program/

[27] https://apstudents.collegeboard.org/what-is-ap

[28] Foster, Richard J. 2010. *Freedom of Simplicity: Revised Edition: Finding Harmony in a Complex World.* New York: HarperCollins. Kindle.

[29] https://www.goarmy.com/rotc/scholarships.html

[30] https://www.afrotc.com/

[31] https://www.nrotc.navy.mil/about.html

[32] https://www.academyadmissions.com/admissions/advice-to-applicants/all-applicants/

[33] https://www.military.com/education/gi-bill/new-post-911-gi-bill-overview.html

[34] https://www.military.com/education/gi-bill/montgomery-gi-bill.html

[35] https://www.military.com/education/gi-bill/selected-reserve-gi-bill-users-guide.html

[36] https://www.military.com/education/gi-bill/vocational-rehabilitation-and-employment-vre.html#eh

[37] https://affordableschools.net/20-tuition-free-colleges/

[38] https://www.nerdwallet.com/blog/loans/student-loans/what-is-work-study/

[39] https://www.cnbc.com/2017/10/04/students-who-work-actually-get-better-grades-but-theres-a-catch.html

[40] https://www.usatoday.com/story/money/columnist/2013/05/25/student-debt-marriage-wedding-loans/2351405/

[41] https://budgeting.thenest.com/debt-affect-marriage-3238.html

[42] https://www.quora.com/What-should-a-college-student-do-over-summer
[43] https://studentaid.ed.gov/sa/types/loans
[44] Ibid
[45] https://studentaid.ed.gov/sa/types/loans/plus
[46] Clark, K. "25 Secrets to Paying for College." CNNMoney.com. April 2012.
[47] https://20somethingfinance.com/education-tax-credits-deductions/
[48] https://www.nerdwallet.com/blog/loans/auto-loans/routine-car-maintenance-cost/
[49] Clark, K. "25 Secrets to Paying for College." CNNMoney.com. April 2012
[50] https://www.usnews.com/news/blogs/data-mine/2014/10/07/student-loan-expectations-myth-vs-reality
[51] https://citadel.abroadoffice.net/fa-q.html
[52] Clark, K. "25 Secrets to Paying for College." CNNMoney.com. April 2012.
[53] https://www.gocoastguard.com/active-duty-careers/officer-opportunities/programs/college-student-pre-commissioning-initiative
[54] https://www.airuniversity.af.edu/Holm-Center/AFROTC/Display/Article/1045423/
[55] https://www.goarmy.com/rotc/college-students.html
[56] https://www.nrotc.navy.mil/scholarships.html
[57] Ibid
[58] http://www.distance-education.org/Articles/Should-You-Take-a-Semester-Off—2009.html
[59] https://studentaid.ed.gov/sa/repay-loans/forgiveness-cancellation/teacher
[60] https://studentaid.ed.gov/sa/repay-loans/forgiveness-cancellation/public-service#qualifying-employment
[61] https://www.bls.gov/emp/tables/employment-by-major-industry-sector.htm
[62] https://www.bls.gov/opub/ted/2018/nonprofits-account-for-12-3-million-jobs-10-2-percent-of-private-sector-employment-in-2016.htm
[63] https://www.studentdebtrelief.us/student-loans/perkins-loan-cancellation/
[64] https://www.studentdebtrelief.us/student-loan-forgiveness/for-nurses/
[65] https://www.studentdebtrelief.us/student-loan-forgiveness/programs/total-and-permanent-disability-discharge/
[66] https://www.studentdebtrelief.us/student-loans/undue-hardship-get-student-loans-discharged-bankruptcy/
[67] https://studentaid.ed.gov/sa/repay-loans/understand/plans/income-driven
[68] https://www.studentdebtrelief.us/student-loan-forgiveness/

[69] https://www.gocoastguard.com/active-duty-careers/officer-opportunities/programs/cspi-student-loan-repayment-program-cspi-slrp

[70] https://world.wng.org/2018/02/repayment_ministry

[71] Burkett, L. 2000. *How to Manage Your Money.* Chicago: Moody.

[72] Ibid

[73] https://www.daveramsey.com/blog/the-truth-about-your-credit-score/

[74] https://www.legalzoom.com/articles/what-happens-if-you-default-on-student-loans

[75] Dayton, H. 2009. Money and Marriage. Chicago: Moody.

[76] Burkett, L. 1990. *The Family Financial Workbook.* Chicago: Moody.

[77] Ibid

[78] https://www.crown.org/blog/ask-chuck-should-my-wife-and-i-have-a-joint-bank-account/

[79] Burkett, L. 1990. *The Family Financial Workbook.* Chicago: Moody.

[80] Ibid

[81] Crown Financial Ministries. 2015. *Do Well—The Crown Biblical Financial Study Manual.* Knoxville: Crown.

[82] https://www.daveramsey.com/blog/gazelle-intensity-do-you-have-it

[83] Ibid

[84] https://www.kiplinger.com

[85] Burkett, L. 1990. *The Family Financial Workbook.* Chicago: Moody.

[86] Ibid

[87] Burkett, Larry. 1994. *The Word on Finances.* Chicago: Moody

[88] Thompson, F.C. 1983. *The Thompson Chain-Reference Bible.* Grand Rapids: Zondervan

[89] https://psychcentral.com/lib/minnesota-multiphasic-personality-inventory-mmpi/

[90] Burkett, L. 1990. *The Family Financial Workbook.* Chicago: Moody.

[91] Bach, David. 2016. *The Automatic Millionaire.* Crown Business: New York.

[92] Stevens, R.H. 2007. *Biblical Perspectives on Money: A Scholastic Study of God's Financial Principles.* Knoxville: Crown.

[93] Burkett, L. 1990. *The Family Financial Workbook.* Chicago: Moody.

[94] Ibid

[95] Stevens, R.H. 2007. *Biblical Perspectives on Money: A Scholastic Study of God's Financial Principles.* Knoxville: Crown.

[96] Burkett, L. 1990. *The Family Financial Workbook.* Chicago: Moody.

About the Author

RUSS STEVENS has degrees in accounting and business and experienced a long stint being trained by and working with Larry Burkett, Christian Financial Concepts, and Crown Financial Ministries. He teaches many of the principles covered in this book in classes as a college professor. Russ also teaches seminars, does speaking engagements, and has led small groups that include these principles. Putting these principles into writing was a joy for him. He loves to see people's lives changed, and God's principles do change lives.

While *Say No! to College Debt* is aimed at students and parents of students, it's also applicable for those going back to or in school later in life (military, career change, advanced degrees, etc.). Russ's other published work, *Biblical Perspectives on Money: A Scholastic Study of God's Principles,* is an academic text useful for teaching many of the same principles.

Russ spent ten years as a contemporary gospel musician in the seminal Jesus Movement group, Children of the Day. The group wrote most of their own material, recorded five albums, and published their music as co-founders/co-sharers of the Maranatha Music label. He now teaches for multiple colleges and universities, reads as much as he can, writes, blogs, and rides his bicycle.

He and his wife, Kathy, enjoy spending time with their four children and seven grandchildren whenever they can get it. They live in the Piedmont region of North Carolina, where they attend a great church. Russ is also active in the praise team at their church and has participated in various levels of leadership.

Russ can be contacted at www.SayNoToCollegeDebt.com or by email at ProfRuss@SayNoToCollegeDebt.com.